Ancient EGYPT

Written by Suzanne Brown
Published by World Teachers Press®

Published with the permission of R.I.C. Publications Pty. Ltd.

Copyright © 2000 by Didax, Inc., Rowley, MA 01969. All rights reserved.

First published by R.I.C. Publications Pty. Ltd., Perth, Western Australia. Revised by Didax Educational Resources.

Distributed in Canada by Scholar's Choice.

Printed in the United States of America.

Order Number 2-5170
ISBN 1-58324-097-7

A B C D E F 03 02 01 00

Educational Resources
395 Main Street
Rowley, MA 01969
www.worldteacherspress.com

Contents

Ancient Egypt provides a comprehensive resource to teachers and students studying this fascinating ancient civilization. The combination of teachers notes, historic information, quality blackline masters and detailed drawings will help bring the history of Egypt to life for both teacher and student.

Suitable for students in grades 4 - 7, *Ancient Egypt* provides a variety of activities that develop skills in many curriculum areas including language, mathematics, history and arts and crafts.

Introduction

Background History

More than 5,000 years ago, Egypt became the first ever nation-state to be united under one king. It was a civilization of great wealth and lasted far longer than either the Greek or Roman civilizations. By the time of Tutankhamun, the pyramids were ancient monuments — more than 1,000 years old.

Egyptians lived in a lush valley along the river banks. Herodotus, the Greek historian, described Egypt as the "Gift of the Nile." A green, fertile tract of land cut its way through the barren Sahara Desert of northeast Africa. Each summer, the Nile flooded, leaving dark, fertile silt over the valley — a gift to the early farmers. The exceptional yield of crops produced a surplus sufficient to support the growing hierarchy of Egyptian society.

The Egyptians were of mixed descent and their culture reflected their African and Semitic ancestry. Their idea of kingship, with its surrounding mythology and regalia, proved to be powerfully effective in managing society as a nation-state. There were occasional upheavels and modifications, but the Egyptian civilization survived for more than 3,000 years.

There were 31 dynasties from the time of Menes, the first ruler of a unified country (3100 B.C.), to Alexander the Great (332 B.C.). The dynasties loosely represent the sequence of ruling families and fell into three main periods — Old Kingdom, Middle Kingdom and New Kingdom.

The King's supreme power reached its height during the Old Kingdom (2686–2181 B.C.). When people built a pyramid for their king, they were proclaiming his divinity and ensuring his eternal life so they could continue to live harmoniously in a land of plenty.

During the 1st Intermediary Period (2181–2040 B.C.), when drought and famine accompanied disunity and civil war, the King's supreme power as divine protector of the people was undermined. Immortality was no longer a royal perogative, but available to all. The king no longer had absolute authority but depended on the goodwill of provincial governors and high priests, who were won over with gifts of land and gold. By the time of the Middle Kingdom (2040–1633 B.C.), the king was more of a wise ruler than a divine power.

By the beginning of the New Kingdom (1570–1070 B.C.), the king had become a war leader. Lesser countries, once in awe of Egypt as an immensely wealthy nation ruled by a deity, forged alliances, and equipped with new sophisticated weapons, challenged Egypt. Warrior pharaohs retaliated and, leading well-trained armies into battle, conquered foreign countries throughout the Near East. Egypt successfully reasserted its authority and built a mighty empire, extending the rays of the sun god, Amun, to all corners of the ancient world.

Ancient Egypt

Teachers Notes

The pictorial map (page 11) reveals the geography of ancient Egypt with the main historical landmarks, including three of the most familiar features: the pyramids (page 13), Tutankhamun's tomb in the Valley of the Kings (page 15) and the temple of Abu Simbel (page 17).

Of the Seven Wonders of the World, only the Great Pyramid of Giza remains. British Egyptologist Howard Carter's discovery of King Tutankhamun's tomb, stacked with treasures, was one of the great archaeological events of the twentieth century. Abu Simbel, the temple of Rameses II, came to prominence in the 1960s when an international engineering endeavor lifted and resited the temple clear of the new flood level set by the Aswan High Dam.

The map covering the extent of foreign trade (page 21) shows Egypt in relation to the other ancient civilizations of the time — Mesopotamia and Syria. Trade inevitably led to an exchange of ideas and skills as well as material goods. Egypt's surplus of grain and gold generated great wealth and helped secure the country's powerful position in the ancient world for more than 3,000 years.

River Nile

Teachers Notes

This section can be introduced by briefly considering the geographical attributes of river valleys across the world.

Extension

1. Use an atlas to locate and follow the course of major rivers of the world – Yangtze, Amazon, Indus, Mississippi, Congo, Ganges, Rhine, Euphrates and Tigris.

2. Consider the nature of rivers; how they flow from high land to low land, are fed by tributaries and cut a course out towards the sea, sometimes traveling for thousands of miles.

3. Consider the benefits to tribespeople of settling on riverbanks and how a river can be a "highway" into the heartland of a continent. The earliest civilizations developed around the river valleys of the Euphrates and Tigris, Indus, Yangtze and Nile.

Egypt's skies are blue and it hardly ever rains but the River Nile waters the land and gives it life. Without the river, the country would be a scorched, sterile desert. The Greek historian, Herodotus, described Egypt as "the gift of the Nile." The ancient Egyptians deified their river and worshipped it as Hapy the Nile god:

"Hail to you O Nile who issues forth from the earth and comes to keep Egypt alive."

They considered their climate a blessing and described other countries as having "a Nile in the sky."

Over the millennia, torrential waters had cut a wide valley through the sandstone plain which, until recently, flooded regularly. The Aswan High Dam (completed in 1971) now controls the floodwaters.

Prehistoric settlers along the banks of the Nile found the flood predictable and reasonably controllable, unlike some rivers, such as the Euphrates, that suddenly broke their banks and changed course, wreaking havoc. Floodwaters brought fine silt downstream, which left a layer of dark mineral-rich mud across the valley floor as the water receded. The flood plain was immensely fertile and contrasted sharply with the waterless wasteland beyond the valley. Egyptians referred to the distinctly different terrains as Kemet, Black Land of the fertile plain and Deshret, Red Land of the surrounding sterile desert.

Farmers' Year

Agriculture spread outwards from the Fertile Crescent in the Near East, where the ancestors of domestic sheep and goat once roamed across plains of wild wheat and barley. Hunters and gatherers harvested the larger seeds, finding them nutritious and easy to store. They kept the best to scatter the following year, and so the art of cultivation developed.

By 8000 B.C., cereal farming had become a way of life around Jericho, and by 5000 B.C. had spread to the Nile valley, where before only wild barley grew. Farmers cultivated several kinds of wheat, barley and legumes. They also grew flax, from which they made linen and extracted linseed oil. Animals were domesticated for their meat, milk and wool and also trained as beasts of burden.

The Nile's alluvial flood plain was naturally fertile. It was rich with wildlife and gave phenomenal crop yields that supported a growing population. There was also a surplus sufficient to feed other groups of people, such as priests and artisans, who were not directly involved in food production, but whose knowledge and skills were highly valued.

By 3000 B.C., the nation state of Egypt was established with a divine king and a ruling elite. They were supported by a surplus of produce, collected from the peasants as tax in exchange for the use of irrigated land. Everything was taxed: cattle, fowl, grain, fruit from orchards and vineyards, and even honey from beehives (see pages 114–115, Early Inventions).

Domestic Life

Most Egyptians lived in rural communities and worked on the land. Many were tenant farmers and rented fields from wealthy landlords or from temple estates. Payment was made in kind with a proportion of produce from the farm.

The poorest people were the peasants, who lived simply in humble dwellings and survived by hiring out their labor. There was no money in ancient Egypt, so wages were paid in basic commodities like sacks of grain, oil for cooking and lighting and lengths of linen. A family could supplement their basic diet of bread and beer, made from wheat and barley, by growing vegetables in the kitchen garden — a small plot of land allocated by the landlord as part of a peasant's wage. Any surplus a family might have could be taken to market and exchanged for other necessities or occasional luxuries.

The Egyptians were fond of animals and were familiar with their ways. Every home had a cat to catch the mice. Cats were revered as the embodiment of Bastet, goddess of love and faithfulness. When a cat died, the grieving family shaved their eyebrows and sometimes had its mummified remains buried at Bastet's temple necropolis in Bubastis.

Egyptian Society

The king was all-powerful. Egypt's fortunes were attributed to him. His word was law. He owned everything and everyone was in his service. Egypt became a nation state on account of the King's divine status. His authority was delegated to officers of state, many of whom were related to him.

But Egypt depended on its peasant farmers who toiled in the fields. Their produce fed the nation. Craftsmen, professionals, nobility and royalty all relied on the surplus produced by the peasants, which was paid in kind as rent to the landlord and tax to the king, leaving just enough to meet their families' basic needs. Coordinating the collection, storage and distribution of the surplus was a considerable task and required a bureaucracy of scribes to keep records and accounts (see pages 32-43, Farmers' Year section).

Religion

Egyptians had many gods and goddesses. Each region had its own deities but some were worshipped throughout the land. Temples were the homes of the gods. The king was their son and through his care he could ensure that harmony and good fortune prevailed throughout the land. Priests carried out the day-to-day temple duties on the King's behalf. They tended the statues of the gods as if they were alive. They dressed and adorned them each morning and offered them food. The statues were cast in gold, which was regarded as a divine metal and the flesh of gods.

Ordinary people did not worship at temples and only saw a statue of a god when it was brought from the temple's innermost shrine and paraded through the town during a festival. Even then it was often shrouded. Every home had its own shrine, with small statues of household deities and busts of family ancestors to protect the home from evil powers.

Ra was the state god for most of Egypt's history, but during the New Kingdom the god Amun of Thebes became prominent. The two gods merged and were worshipped as Amun-Ra. The main cult center shifted from Heliopolis (city of the sun) to Thebes. An image of Amun led the Egyptian army across the ancient world. Imperial victories were attributed to his power. Tributes from defeated countries poured into Amun's temple near Thebes, making it the wealthiest in the world and its priests immensely powerful.

Afterlife

From the earliest days, the dead were buried in pits dug in the desert. The poor continued to be buried in this way throughout Egyptian civilization. The hot, dry sand naturally desiccated and preserved the body from decay, but if it was laid to rest in a stone or mud brick tomb it tended to decompose. The art of embalming developed to preserve the body, for Egyptians believed a person could only have an afterlife if the body was mummified. Embalmers used natron, a naturally occurring salt, which simulated the effect of the dry desert sand.

Egyptians imagined that when a person died several souls left the body. The most important were the Ka, Ba and Akh. The Ka lived on in the mummy and depended on food offerings for nourishment. The Ba, usually represented as a bird with a human head, wandered freely, often with flocks of other souls, but it always returned to the body. It was the Ba that made the perilous journey through the Underworld and faced judgment in the Hall of Truth. The Akh left the body entirely, to shine among the stars or join the crew of Ra's Day Boat, as a blessed soul.

Artisan's Tomb

Teachers Notes

This section provides ideas and information to help make and decorate a model tomb, complete with funerary goods.

Rock-cut tombs, popular throughout Egyptian civilization, honeycombed the cliffs of the Western Desert. Situated high above the flood plain of the valley they provided a safe resting place for the dead. A tomb was the "House of the Ka" and contained provisions for the afterlife. Favorite possessions were often included, like a beloved toy, keepsake or souvenir. Wall paintings often depicted food production such as farming, herding, baking and brewing to ensure an everlasting provision for the dead person's Ka.

Egyptians imagined tomb paintings came to life by magic but it was better if the real thing or a model was placed in the tomb. The wealthy, wishing to take their valuables with them, filled their tombs with much of the finest work produced by Egypt's craftsmen. The greater the luxuries, the greater the risk of tomb robbers. Most tombs have been ransacked and nearly everything of value carried off, but the dry desert climate has helped preserve what was left and many wall paintings remain in pristine condition. A number of tombs have provided archaeologists with invaluable time capsules describing life in ancient Egypt 3,000 years ago. (See pages 62–63, Archaeological Evidence and pages 14–15, Tutankhamun's Tomb)

Jewelry

Teachers Notes

This section is introduced with an example of one of the most familiar and elaborate pieces of royal jewelry ever discovered, and is followed by a sequence of activity sheets giving guidelines for making a range of jewelry suitable for dressing up.

Both men and women wore jewelry in many forms — necklaces, collars and pectorals or pendants, bracelets, rings, armlets, anklets, girdles and headdresses. The bold, colorful designs of Egyptian jewelry complemented the simple white linen clothing.

Gold was much sought after for making jewelry. It was supreme among metals, never tarnishing or corroding and having the fiery glow of the Sun. It was considered the flesh of the gods.

Valuable gold jewelry was made by court craftsmen for the king so he could reward his loyal subjects. One of the oldest honors was the "Order of the Golden Collar," ceremoniously presented and hung around the neck of favored officials. The "Order of the Golden Fly" was frequently awarded for bravery. Owning gold conveyed status, wealth and power in an age when there was no money.

Gold was easily worked by beating and embossing with simple tools. It was also cast in molds and inlaid with gemstones. The favorites were red carnelian, found as pebbles in the Eastern Desert, turquoise, from the Sinai Desert, and deep blue lapis lazuli imported from faraway Afghanistan along ancient trade routes (see pages 18–21, Foreign Trade). These three colors, together with gold, gave Egyptian jewelry its classic quality.

Introduction

Gold was abundant in Nubia and the Eastern Desert. Shining gold granules were found in the sand of dried-up river beds. It was also mined from hard quartz rock by labor gangs of captives, criminals and soldiers working under guard, often in appalling conditions. Over time the mines were slowly exhausted. Gold became increasingly inaccessible and the supply diminished.

On account of tomb robbers, an increasing problem in the New Kingdom, funerary jewelry made from colored glass and plaster with gold leaf overlay became commonplace, even in royal tombs.

Hieroglyphs

Egyptians described hieroglyphs as "the words of go." They believed Thoth, the ibis-headed god, had given them the gift of writing and had also written the books containing all the knowledge of the world. A scribe always started writing by first pouring a libation from his water pot in honor of Thoth, who was the patron god of scribes.

The idea of writing appears to have originated in Mesopotamia and probably emerged from the use of seals on merchandise to denote ownership. Writing was fundamental to the smooth running of the Egyptian state. Scribes, working from numerous mud huts dotted along the banks of the Nile, organized society by keeping records and inventories, assessing taxes and writing letters. They had adequate calculating skills for surveying land and estimating quantities of building materials (see pages 54–63, Egyptian Society).

The clay tablet, which Babylonians used for writing, was superseded by Egyptian papyrus. It was exported across the ancient world until the 8th century A.D., when cloth paper was introduced from the Orient.

The Greeks called the signs carved in stone on temple walls hieroglyphs meaning "sacred inscriptions." They were often highly decorative, painted in brilliant colors on white plastered tomb walls, inlaid in colored glass on coffin lids and embossed in fine detail on sheet gold. A simplified form of hieroglyphic writing developed for everyday tasks of writing letters and keeping accounts. It was called hieratic and was more suited to the flow of a reed pen on papyrus. With time, further refinement produced an even simpler cursive form called demotic. Few samples of these scripts remain, having long since crumbled away in the damp soil of towns along the valley. In the dry, dark tombs of the desert hills, however, many fragile funerary papyri survived for thousands of years.

Egypt became a Roman province in 30 B.C. and the temple schools were eventually closed. The last known stone carved hieroglyphs were made at the temple of Isis on the island of Philae in A.D. 394. It was not long after that the meaning of hieroglyphs was forgotten.

Teachers Notes
Features and sites in bold print can be located on the map (page 11).

Extension
Compare the pictorial map shown here with a geographical map.

Egypt extends as an oasis along the lush, green river valley of the Nile from the **First Cataract**, on the border with **Nubia**, down-river to the sluggish waters of the marshy **Delta** on the **Mediterranean coast**. The natural boundaries of Egypt gave considerable protection from invasion. Beyond the valley is the **Western Desert** and **Eastern Desert**. To the north is the **Mediterranean Sea** and to the south, the unnavigable rocky rapids of the First Cataract. Trade from tropical Africa passed through the Nubian border, via a canal, at the frontier town of **Aswan**.

Both the pyramids and the **Valley of the Kings** are royal burial sites. The **Great Pyramids of Giza** are close to **Memphis**, the capital during the Old Kingdom. The Valley of the Kings lies in the desert hills beyond the west bank opposite **Thebes**, the capital of the New Kingdom. The position of the burial sites reflects the shift in the center of power from **Lower Egypt** to **Upper Egypt** after the first 1,500 years of Egyptian civilization.

Pilgrims journeyed up and down the Nile to cult centers of major deities. Ra Atum, the sun god, was worshipped at **Heliopolis**, Osiris, god of the Underworld, at **Abydos**, and his wife, the goddess Isis, at her island temple of **Philae**. At **Crocodilopolis**, in the **Faiyum Oasis**, sacred crocodiles lolled in the temple pools. In the Delta at **Bubastis** was the temple of the cat goddess Bastet. Mummified cats were buried in the necropolis. The temple of Amun at Thebes became the wealthiest of all time.

In 332 B.C., Alexander the Great, after liberating Egypt from Persian rule, founded the city of **Alexandria** on the Mediterranean coast. It flourished as the cultural and economic center of the ancient world. The **Pharos Lighthouse** in the harbor of Alexandria was one of the Seven Wonders of the World. It was completed in 260 B.C.

Color the fertile regions, along the banks of the Nile, green, the desert bordering the valley, yellow, and the river and sea, blue.

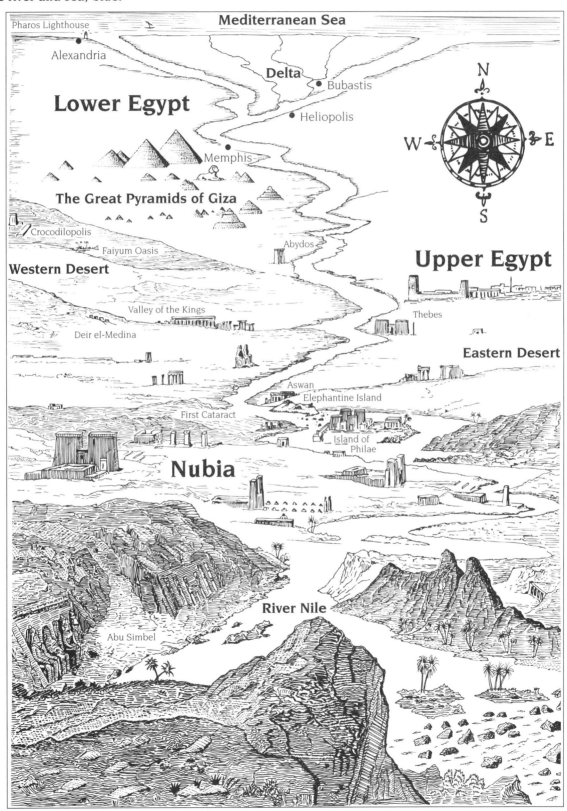

Teachers Notes

Consider the great scale of the pyramids and the purpose for which they were built.

Extension

1. Monumental public works, such as temples and city walls, are an expression of every civilization. What public buildings are there in your area?

2. The Great Pyramids of Giza stand on the edge of the desert to the west of the Nile, the Land of the Dead. Using cut black paper silhouettes, make a picture of the sun setting over the pyramids.

3. Consider how the following people helped build the pyramids.

    stonemasons   quarrymen   overseers   scribes   architects

    astronomers   surveyors   laborers   artists   ferrymen   engineers

4. Consider how the Egyptians:
    (a) achieved a level site by reference to the water level in a network of channels cut into the rock across the site. This could be investigated by exploring how water finds its own level. Use a U-tube or cut channels through mud from high to low ground.
    (b) surveyed true square foundations (see pages 108–109, Measures).
    (c) maneuvered heavy blocks. Use bricks to demonstrate how friction can be reduced by:
        i. spreading a layer of slippery mud between bricks; or
        ii. pulling a brick along over pencil "rollers."
        Measure the reduction of friction with a spring balance on the level and also up "ramps."

The stepped pyramid was designed by the genius Imhotep, for King Djoser around 2650 B.C. It was the first monumental stone building in the world. Until then mud bricks had been used.

The Age of Pyramids lasted around 1,000 years and marked the expression of Egypt as a nation state. Building a pyramid took many years and was an enormous achievement in organization, requiring cooperation between the people of both Lower and Upper Egypt. It was a tribute to their protector, the divine king. Encased in white limestone blocks, the pyramids rose above the desert plain, shimmering like the sun's rays breaking through low clouds. The gilded capstones, fashioned in gold from the Eastern Desert, glinted with the first rays of the morning sun.

Many different trades were engaged in the building work. Astronomers took sightings from the stars to determine near-perfect alignment of the sides of the pyramids with the cardinal points. Surveyors established a level foundation using a grid of channels filled with water. Engineers calculated load bearings to redistribute the mass of stonework, which otherwise would have caused the pyramids to collapse. Peasant farmers were conscripted as the labor force during the hot summer months, when the fields were flooded and farming was lax. Ferrymen transported huge granite blocks used for lining the pyramids 805 km downriver from quarries at Aswan.

The flood plain extended to the desert edge where the pyramids were sited, so stone could be transported to the site by barge during the annual flood.

Size of Pyramids

		height	base			height	base
1.	Khufu	146 m	230 m	2.	Menkaura	66 m	104 m
3.	Djoser	59 m	115 m	4.	Sahura	43 m	78 m
5.	Sneferu	96 m	143 m				

The Great Pyramid of King Khufu covers an area equivalent to seven or eight football fields.

"A stairway to the sky has been set up for him so that he might ascend the heaven thereby." *Pyramid texts.*

The pyramids were the tombs of kings. Each one took thousands of men many years to build. They were designed to reach up to heaven so the king could take his place with the gods among the stars.

Look at the silhouette of each pyramid. Use the scale to calculate the height and length of the sides of each pyramid. Make a set of models of the pyramids drawn to scale.

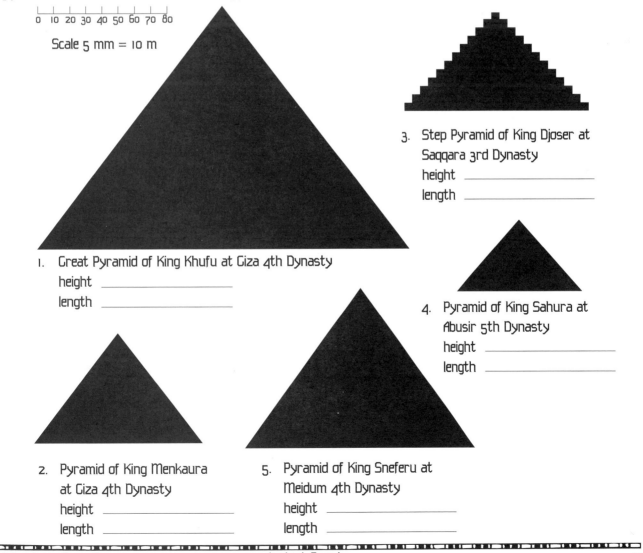

0 10 20 30 40 50 60 70 80

Scale 5 mm = 10 m

3. Step Pyramid of King Djoser at Saqqara 3rd Dynasty

height _____

length _____

1. Great Pyramid of King Khufu at Giza 4th Dynasty

height _____

length _____

4. Pyramid of King Sahura at Abusir 5th Dynasty

height _____

length _____

2. Pyramid of King Menkaura at Giza 4th Dynasty

height _____

length _____

5. Pyramid of King Sneferu at Meidum 4th Dynasty

height _____

length _____

Teachers Notes

Writing a news release on the discovery of Tutankhamun's tomb could provide an exercise in desktop publishing.

Vocabulary:	excavation	tomb	Egyptologist	archaeologist
	necropolis	annex	antechamber	treasury

Extension

1. Write a story, "Last Days of Tutankhamun."

2. Research the contents of Tutankhamun's tomb.
   Make a collage of the treasures stacked in the antechamber.

3. Make the nemes headcloth of Tutankhamun (see page 98, Extension 1).

4. Make a model of a rock cut tomb (see pages 80-81, Chapel and Tomb).

Kings were buried in pyramids until the beginning of the New Kingdom; after that they were buried in rock-cut tombs across the river from Thebes, in a secret place called the Valley of the Kings. Tutankhamun was buried here. He died at the age of 18 after two days of fever following a head injury near his left ear. His cause of death remains a mystery. It could have been an accident or battle injury, possibly even assassination.

His tomb was not ready so he was buried in an existing nobleman's tomb, which was modest for royalty. Two mummified fetuses were found in his tomb, possibly his stillborn children. He had been married to Ankhesenamun, who was probably his younger half-sister. He left no successor.

Tutankhamun had succeeded the heretic pharaoh, Akhenaten who, with his wife, the beautiful Nefertiti, had incurred the wrath of the wealthy priesthood by closing the temples and commanding by decree the worship of only one god, Aten the Sun god. After Akhenaten's death in 1333 B.C., the eight-year-old pharaoh was crowned Tutankhaten, "the living image of Aten." With his guardian's help, he soon reopened the old temples that had been closed for over 20 years, taking the name Tutankhamun, "the living image of Amun." The priests returned to their worship of Amun of Thebes and with it their old, lucrative way of life.

"Surely never before in the whole history of excavation had such an amazing sight been seen."
Archaeologist, Howard Carter, discovering the lost tomb of Tutankhamun in November, 1922.

 Read the notes based on Carter's account then write a news release.

Tutankhamun's tomb discovered 3,000 years since feet trod here.

Place – Valley of the Kings.
Royal necropolis of 30 kings.
Rock-cut tombs in deserted Theban hills on west bank of the Nile.

Date – 1917
Carter begins excavation in search of lost tomb of boy king, Tutankhamun – died aged 18 years.

Sponsor – Lord Carnarvon, amateur Egyptologist.

King Tutankhamun's Burial Mask

Plan of King Tutankhamun's Tomb

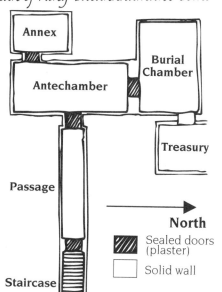

November 4, 1922
Workmen uncover steps leading down to sealed doorway.
"We were preparing to leave the Valley and try our luck elsewhere and then – hardly had we set hoe to ground in our last despairing effort than we made a discovery that far exceeded our wildest dreams."

November 26, 1922
Last of rubble cleared from passageway. Carter makes a hole in doorway and peers into candlelit antechamber.
"As my eyes grew accustomed to the light, details of the room within emerged slowly from the mist; strange animals, statues and gold – everywhere the glint of gold."

Teachers Notes

The cloze comprehension introduces the warrior pharaoh Rameses II and his great claim to fame. The illustration is based on a water color from the works of David Roberts, an 18th century explorer. He documented the monuments of Egypt before the days of photography.

Cloze passage answers:

warrior, colossal, border, rock, statues, hall, gods, sun, temple, battle, chariot, victory, escape, valley, water, world

Extension

1. Estimate the height of the seated statues of Rameses II using one of the people in the picture as a unit of measure.

2. What kind of person do you imagine Rameses II to have been? Why do you think such an imposing temple was built in Nubia beyond the Egyptian border?

The Hittites were a warring nation who occupied present-day Turkey. They threatened the northern border of the Egyptian empire. Qadesh was a city state near the border.

Almost every temple in Egypt portrays a superhuman Rameses II boasting of his great personal courage in battle. However, the Hittites' version of the battle of Qadesh claims Rameses II was not only defeated but also lost territory. Soon after, in 1274 B.C., the warring countries signed the first recorded peace treaty. Neither side could afford to continue with expensive military campaigns. Egyptian gold mines were exhausted and the empire was in decline. Rameses II married two Hittite princesses, which helped to keep the peace.

He reigned for more than 60 years and had more than 100 wives and 150 children.

🔺 **Use the words below to help you complete the passage.**

rock	sun
border	valley
gods	statues
warrior	hall
battle	victory
water	temple
colossal	chariot
world	escape

Rameses II was the last of the great _____ kings. Throughout the land,

_____ statues and temples still stand in his memory. Abu Simbel is the most

famous. It lies beyond Egypt's _____ in Nubia and was carved out of the solid

_____ of a cliff face overlooking the Nile.

Four gigantic _____ of Rameses II sit alongside each other. Between them the

temple entrance opens into a great _____ with more statues of Rameses II together

with his favorite _____ . Twice a year the rays of the rising

_____ illuminate the statues within.

The _____ walls are covered with scenes from the Battle of Qadesh. Rameses II

boasted of winning the _____ single-handedly. He is seen in his

_____ charging the enemy with the horse's reins tied around his waist. But it was

not the great _____ he would have liked. It was more of a lucky

_____ !

In 1962, the Aswan High Dam was built and the Nubian _____ was flooded; but first

the temple of Abu Simbel was cut into huge pieces and lifted high up above the new

_____ level. Engineers came from all over the _____ to help

with the project.

Teachers Notes

The activities require students be given pages 19 and 21 together. The exotic nature of Egypt's trade is illustrated.

The map work focuses on ancient trade routes across the Middle East. Consider the vast areas of difficult terrain covered by traders of the ancient world.

Extension

1. Imagine yourself a trader in ancient times crossing either desert or sea. Write a story about one of your expeditions.

2. Explore the Egyptian empire. Egyptians established a vast empire with horses, chariots and weapons, previously introduced by Hyksos invaders from the east. At its height, under the reign of Thutmose III, the empire extended across Sinai into Syria, up to the Euphrates river and also south into Nubia.

3. Shade the trade map to illustrate the extent of the Egyptian empire.

The state controlled foreign trade and received all the revenue which, together with tributes from conquered lands and income from local taxes, made Egypt the wealthiest country in the ancient world.

An Assyrian king demands gold from his friend, the king of Egypt –
"Gold in your country is as common as dirt. One simply gathers it up.
Why then do you keep it all for yourself? I am building myself a new
palace so send me as much gold as I will need for its adornment.
If your purpose is one of true friendship you will send me much gold."

The illustration of the trading ship is based on stone carvings in Hatshepsut's temple recording the legendary expedition to the land of Punt.

Peasants in Egypt lived a simple life, but the rich enjoyed all kinds of luxuries brought from far and wide.

 Number the picture of Nubians bringing exotic gifts from tropical Africa to the Egyptian court.

1. giraffe tails
2. monkey
3. basket of fruit
4. ivory tusks
5. baboon
6. gold rings
7. leopard skin
8. ebony logs
9. ostrich feathers

The gold mines in the Eastern Desert and Nubia brought Egypt great wealth. Foreigners wanted gold to decorate their palaces and temples. In exchange, Egypt received timber for building boats and copper for making tools.

 Look at the map to help you answer the questions.

1. From where did Egypt import timber? _____

2. From where did Egypt import copper? _____

3. What goods did Egypt export? _____

 Mark the trade routes described in the following passage on the map.

Ancient people traveled great distances across the sea and the desert in search of treasures.

Queen Hatshepsut sent an expedition along the eastern coast of Africa to the land of Punt in search of myrrh and frankincense. A fleet of ships had to be carried from the Nile right across the desert to the Red Sea before setting sail to the land of Punt.

Nomads brought a dark blue precious gemstone called lapis lazuli all the way from the mountains in Afghanistan. They traveled with their caravans of donkeys across deserts and over mountains to Babylon in Mesopotamia. Traders carried the lapis lazuli up the Euphrates River valley, then across to the port of Byblos in Syria. From here it was sent to countries all around the Mediterranean.

See page 18 for Foreign Trade background information and teachers notes.

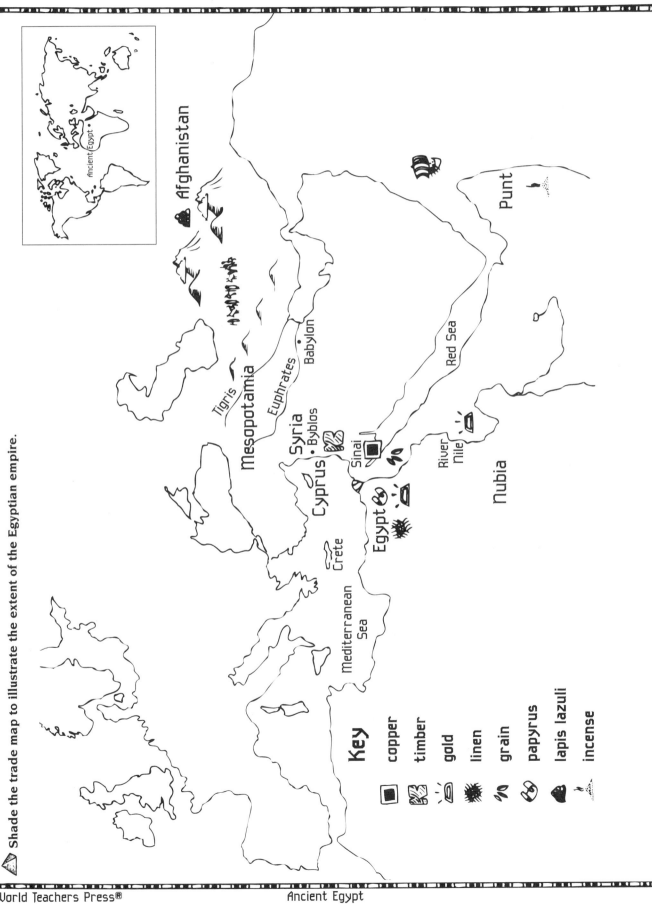

Shade the trade map to illustrate the extent of the Egyptian empire.

Afghanistan

Punt

Mesopotamia

Tigris

Euphrates

Babylon

Syria

Byblos

Cyprus

Sinai

Red Sea

River Nile

Nubia

Egypt

Crete

Mediterranean Sea

Key

copper

timber

gold

linen

grain

papyrus

lapis lazuli

incense

Teachers Notes

The frieze portrays how Egyptian life has always been closely bound to the rivers.

Note: When coloring the scene, only the lowland is green and fertile, the upper land is barren desert.

Extension

1. Daily life along the river bank, seen from a boat, can be presented as a story board.

2. Consider modern-day life on the banks of the Nile compared to the past.

3. Make a shoe box theater. Enlarge the frieze with a photocopier. Insert dowel rollers through the shoe box. Cut a suitably sized window in the lid and wind the frieze onto rollers. Present with a commentary.

Upper Egypt remains essentially rural. The river is central to the life of the people. Networks of canals and ditches stretch across the valley carrying water to a patchwork of small fields. Now the land no longer floods and farmers must rely on added fertilizers to maintain crop yields. Operating a shadoof is strenuous work and has now been largely replaced by electric pumps.

People still fill their drinking vessels from the Nile's clear water, though infectious parasites abound. Cattle and sheep are driven down to the water's edge to drink and are also ferried to islands in the marshes for fresh grazing. Laden donkeys follow tracks beside the river. Innumerable water fowl shelter in the reed beds and little egrets gather around the moored boats.

There is no longer any danger from crocodiles and hippopotamuses, which are now extinct in Egypt's stretch of the Nile. The papyrus is also extinct, but people continue to cut reeds for thatching and making windbreaks around their crops. Shady walled gardens surround dwellings and people rest in the shade of the palm groves, living among the remains of an ancient civilization. The tall pylons of a crumbling temple can be seen from the water alongside the mosque of modern-day Egypt.

Most Egyptians lived close to the banks of the Nile. They often traveled by boat to market or to visit temples on festival days. Sometimes they went on long pilgrimages to the temples of their favorite gods.

Color, cut out and join the strips together to make a frieze showing a short journey from a village to a nearby temple. On a separate piece of paper, write a commentary.

Glue behind next picture.

Glue behind next picture.

Glue behind next picture.

Teachers Notes

The series of pictures illustrates the variety and extent of river transport. Instructions are given for making a papyrus skiff.

Extension

1. Look for pictures of tomb paintings of noblemen on family outings in the marshes, hunting fish and wildfowl from their papyrus skiffs, with spears and throwing sticks. Make a large collage for a wall display titled "Hunting in the Marshes," based on the tomb paintings (see page 25).

2. Find out about the different uses of papyrus. Draw a series of pictures to illustrate the things Egyptians made. These include paper (the word comes from papyrus), thatching and canopies, mats, rope, baskets, stools, sieves and sandals.

3. Investigate flotation. Find the load limit of different vessels.

4. Consider other kinds of transportation in Egypt. Egyptians were the first to domesticate donkeys as beasts of burden, carrying loads along pathways between fields and villages. Horses, introduced by the invading Hyksos around 1640 B.C., were used by noblemen for war chariots and hunting expeditions in the desert. Camels eventually reached Egypt when the Persians invaded around 500 B.C.

How were boats powered?

Traveling north, boats drifted downstream with the strong current, often helped by oarsmen. Traveling south was against the current but, by raising large square sails, boats could use the strong prevailing wind from the north. The hieroglyph for traveling north is a boat with the sail down and for traveling south a boat with the sail up (see page 113, Hieroglyphs).

When were sailing boats first used?

The earliest record of a sailing boat comes from a decorated pot more than 5,000 years old.

What materials were used for boat building?

Lengths of papyrus were bound together to make quite substantial rafts. Short lengths of wood were cut from acacia and sycamore and tied together with papyrus rope. Egypt was short of good timber so long, straight pieces needed for shipbuilding were imported from the cedar forests of Lebanon (see pages 18–21, Foreign Trade).

Why was river transportation so important in ancient Egypt?

It is far easier to float a heavy load over water than haul it over land. Egypt's monumental building works depended on Nile transportation. Obelisks, weighing up to 110 tons, cut from granite at Aswan were transported downstream on 61 meter barges towed by fleets of rowing boats. Pillars for temples and the lining stone for the pyramids were also brought from Aswan. The journey to Memphis took one to two weeks, depending on the current.

The Nile made communication the length of Egypt possible, which was essential for keeping contact and coordinating projects and campaigns across regions.

Cargoes of all kinds, including livestock, were common. Trade and tax collection depended on river transportation. Funeral barges carried coffins from the east to west banks.

The River Nile was like a highway. Boats were very much a part of the Egyptian way of life.

Look at these pictures of boats, taken from Egyptian tomb paintings. Describe the different types of Nile boats.

See page 24 for Nile Boats and Papyrus Skiff background information and teachers notes.

The first boats were papyrus skiffs made from bundles of reeds lashed together with rope.

 Make a model of a papyrus skiff.
You will need:

- scissors
- thin string
- darning needle or bodkin
- bundle of reeds 30 – 40 cm long

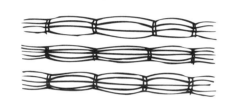

1. Make three bundles of reeds. Tie them together with string.

2. Sew the bundles together to make a raft.

3. Make two longer bundles for the sides of the skiff.

4. Sew the sides to the raft of shorter reeds.

5. Tie off the ends of the outer bundles leaving two lengths of string. Trim the ends of the reeds.

6. Bend up both stern and bow to give shape to the skiff. Hold in place by securing the ends of the string to the base of the raft.

Teachers Notes

Having deduced the principle of raising water by using a beam pivoted with a counterweight, students need to select appropriate materials to design and make a working model.

Extension

1. Using mud or clay, investigate irrigation techniques.
   (a) Make catch basins and channels.
   (b) Use model shadoofs to raise water from low to high levels.
   (c) Divert water with dams or sluices.

2. Model of the Nile.
   Build up the contours of a river valley on a large tray or water-containing vessel. Line with plastic sheeting and cover with sand, sealed with glue. Use acrylic to paint the "river" blue and fields green, leaving the high land as sandy desert. Line the water edge with papyrus clumps set in modeling clay. Position papyrus skiffs (page 27), shadoofs (page 29), mud brick dwellings (page 45) and pyramids (page 13). Add paper-cut palms and modeling clay animals. Experiment with flooding and draining the fields. Sow "crops" of alfalfa.

Receding floodwater was retained in catch basins and released over the year into canals by lifting sluice gates. However, hand-filled pots still had to be carried on yokes for watering gardens of vines and fruit trees.

Reclaiming low-lying land greatly increased the agricultural output of the nation. The canal network was extended into the barren desert beyond the flood plain, and marshland was brought under cultivation by maintaining drainage ditches.

Irrigation has always been fundamental to Egypt's agricultural prosperity. Complex irrigation schemes for controlling the river required extensive knowledge and skill in hydraulic engineering. Menes, the first king of Egypt, was depicted cutting a new canal. Canal building was a major undertaking of the state and depended on cooperation and coordination between regions. Like any massive public building works, irrigation schemes unified the country in a common purpose. As part of their labor tax to the king, gangs of peasants were recruited as laborers for digging canals. Water rights were enforceable by law and many punishable crimes were related to their infringement. At the final judgment in the underworld the dead soul had to swear he had not diverted his neighbor's water (see pages 76-77, Weighing of the Heart, and pages 36–37, The Flood).

It hardly ever rains in Egypt. Egyptians have always depended on the Nile for watering their crops.

They diverted water from the river to the fields along a network of canals and ditches. The Egyptians built catch basins and dams to hold back the floodwater.

They also invented a device called a shadoof to help them raise water from one level to another.

Shadoofs are still being used in some parts of Egypt.

**Look at the pictures of a shadoof.
Describe how you think it works.**

_____

_____

_____

_____

_____

_____

_____

_____

_____

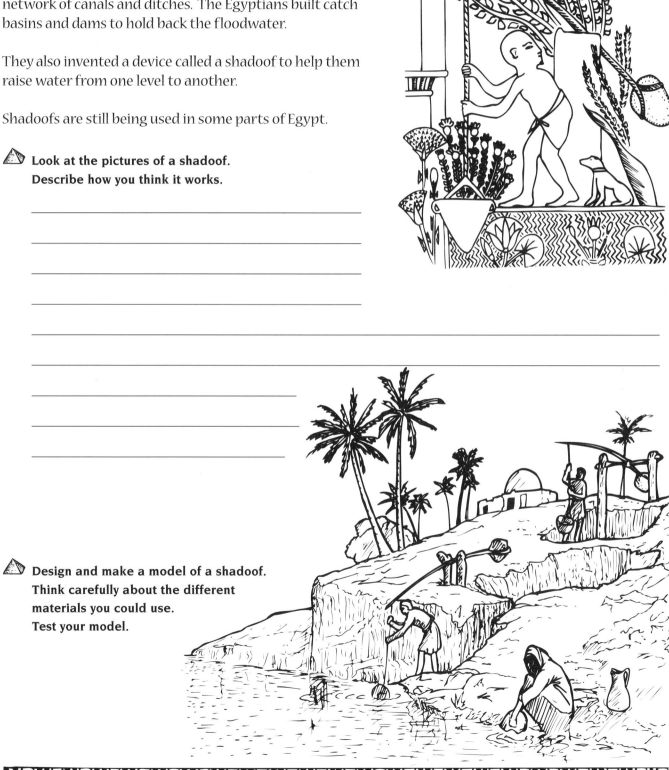

**Design and make a model of a shadoof.
Think carefully about the different
materials you could use.
Test your model.**

Teachers Notes

The source of the Nile and the cause of the annual flood are considered and contrasted with the ancient Egyptians' mythological explanation. The cloze comprehension is completed by referring to the map.

Cloze passage answers:

Victoria, River, Blue, Khartoum, Nile, Ethiopian Highlands, Egypt, delta, Mediterranean, Nile, Aswan High Dam, Nubia, Nasser

Extension

1. What modern-day countries does the Nile flow through? Use an atlas to help you find out.

2. Estimate the size of Lake Victoria from the map. Find out about the 19th century explorers in Africa and how Lake Victoria came to be named.

3. Consider some of the advantages and disadvantages of the Aswan High Dam.

   Advantages: Control of flood waters and hydro-electric power.

   Disadvantages: Silt is no longer deposited so fertilizers now have to be added to the soil. Waterborne diseases, including bilharzia carried by water snails, increase with stagnant water.

The distance from Lake Victoria to the Mediterranean Sea is approximately 6,500 km. The Nile is one of the longest rivers in the world.

The mineral-rich silt that once regularly fertilized the flood plain had been scoured by raging floods from the rocky Ethiopian Highlands during the monsoons and carried in the turbulent waters downstream for thousands of miles. As the waters slowed, the silt was deposited across the valley floor on either side of the Nile. Since the building of the Aswan High Dam (1971) the floodwaters are held back and fertile silt no longer reaches the valley.

Egyptians believed the Nile flowed from a rocky cavern beneath an island at Aswan, where Hapy the river god lived, and that each year the Nile flooded with the tears of the goddess Isis mourning for Osiris, her dead husband. Egyptians celebrated the flood in a great festival called the "Night of the Tear Drop."

Nineteenth century explorers eventually discovered the sources of the Nile and found out why it flooded every year. Following the Nile southwards for thousands of miles, they arrived at snow-capped mountains, tropical swamps and a vast freshwater lake.

▲ **Estimate the length of the Nile.**

▲ **Look at the map and then complete the passage.**

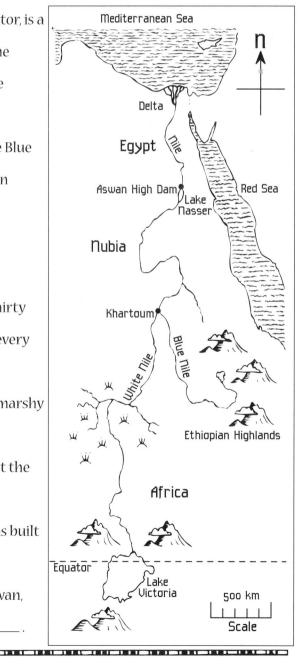

Lake _____ , on the equator, is a

natural reservoir fed by summer rains. It gently feeds into the

_____ Nile through the year. The White Nile

meets the _____ Nile at the modern city of

_____ . Every year in May, the Blue

_____ swells to a seething mass of muddy brown

water. Melting snow and monsoon rains in the

_____

_____ sweep down the

mountain gullies, scouring silt from the rocks. Until about thirty

years ago the river valley in _____ flooded every

summer.

A dark, rich silt was left behind. The water flowed on to the marshy

_____ and out to the

_____ Sea, but the

_____ no longer floods in Egypt. The

_____ _____ _____ was built

to hold back and control the flood. The ancient country of

_____ on the banks of the Nile, south of Aswan,

now lies beneath the water of Lake _____ .

Teachers Notes

Rotating the calendar wheel counterclockwise reveals the annual rise and fall of the Nile and the different seasonal activities. Students need pages 33 and 35 to make the calendar wheel.

Extension

1. Referring to the calendar wheel, make a table showing all the different kinds of work done in each season.

2. How is the ancient Egyptians' calendar different from ours? Make a calendar wheel for our cycle of seasons.

Egypt's climate favored cultivation. The Nile flooded the valley during the hottest months of the year. By October, the floodwater had receded and was followed by a temperate winter, which was the growing season. Crops ripened during the drought of the spring months from March to May.

New Year was celebrated in mid-July when the harvest was in, the drought was over and the river was rising.

The farming year had a cycle of three seasons.

Akhet   The time of inundation, when the fields were flooded. For up to three months no work could be done on the land. Peasants were recruited as laborers to work on building projects including the pyramids and temples.

Peret   At the time of emergence, when the fields reappeared, flood damage was fixed. This included repairing ditches and dikes and replacing dislodged boundary stones. Fields were plowed and seed was sown. The plow scratched the surface, just sufficient to break up the hard pan of sun-baked silt without drying out the soil.

Shemu   The time of drought, when the fields were baked dry by the sun, gardens needed constant watering. Peasants worked hard to collect the harvest before the floods came in the New Year.

Use Calendar Wheel sheets 1 and 2 to make a calendar wheel. You will need:

- glue
- paper fastener
- tape
- stapler
- crayons
- two pieces of thin cardboard (20 cm² and 42 x 24 cm)

1. Cut out the circle below and the square on page 35.
2. Glue both onto cardboard and score (a).
3. Cut out the wheel and shaded areas on the square.
4. Fold the sleeve.
5. Color the pictures.
6. Make a small hole through the centers.
7. Assemble with a paper fastener and tape down flap (b) as shown.
8. Rotate the circle to find what happened in each season.

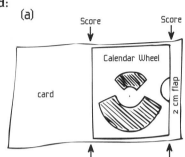

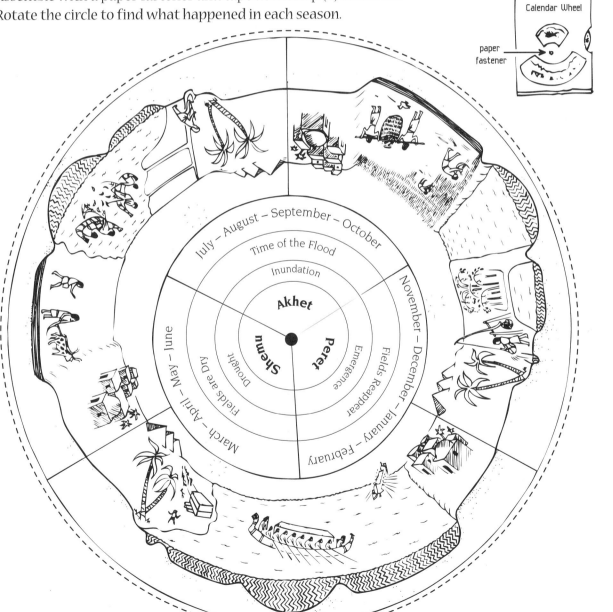

See page 32 for Calendar Wheel background information and teachers notes.

Egyptian Calendar Wheel

The Three Seasons

Akhet	Season of Inundation
Peret	Season of Emergence
Shemu	Season of Drought

New Year's Day was July 19. This was the time when the River Nile began to flood. The fields lay under water all summer. In the temperate winter, when the floods had gone, the crops grew. By spring, they were ready for harvesting.

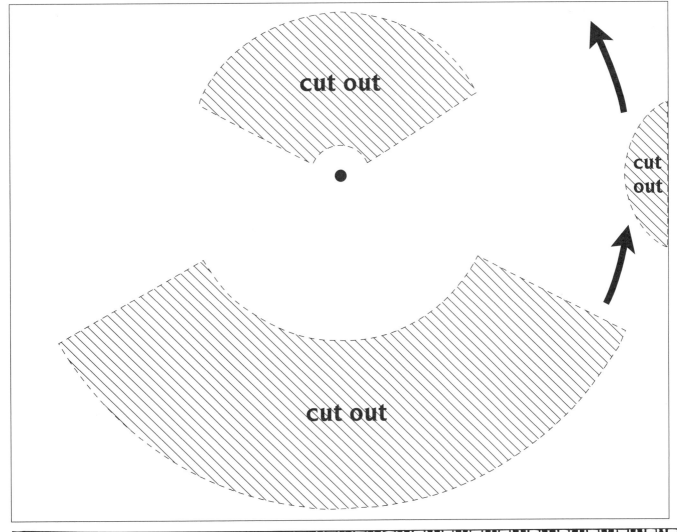

Teachers Notes
The impact of the flood on village life is considered as well as the consequences of a high or low flood.

Extension

1. Consider how water levels in local rivers and streams change over the year (see pages 108–109, Measures).

2. When and where have you ever seen floods? Consider the damage a flood can cause.

3. Make a graph showing the change in water levels on the Nile recorded over one year, earlier this century, before the Aswan High Dam was built:

May – 1.0 m	June – 0.8 m	July – 3.2 m	August – 7.0 m
September – 9.0 m	October – 7.6 m	November – 5.0 m	December – 2.3 m
January – 2.0 m	February – 1.6 m	March – 1.0 m	April – 1.0 m

   Cross-check graph with the illustrated calendar wheel (see pages 32–35, Calendar Wheel 1 and 2).

4. Imagine you are a District Governor in Upper Egypt and nilometer readings predict the New Year will bring the highest floods in living memory. Make contingency plans for your district. Consider evacuating villagers from their homes, relocating local granaries, caring for livestock, repositioning dikes and diverting floodwaters.

5. Famine
   (a) There were times during the history of Egyptian civilization when the pattern of climate changed. A series of low floods could bring drought and famine. In their wisdom, overseers of state granaries prepared for lean years by stockpiling grain. (Find out about Joseph's interpretation of the pharaoh's dream prophesying famine.)

   (b) Egypt's fortunes were tied to the Nile. During the Intermediate Period around 2000 B.C., there was an extensive drought and grain stores became depleted. A series of kings, each ruling for only a year or two, failed to restore the flood levels. People were dying of famine, temples and tombs were ransacked and civil war broke out. It was apparent the king had lost control of the Nile and its fertile valley. His divine status and supreme power were in question. Corruption and bribery became rife, state control broke down and the country degenerated into a series of feuding regions. (Consider conditions in countries of the modern-day world where there is famine.)

   (c) Egyptian mythology describes how, on one occasion when there was a severe drought, the wise King Djoser appeased Khnum, god of the flood and silt, by decreeing that one-tenth of all harvest produce should be offered to Khnum at his temple on the island of Elephantine near the southern border, from where the flood was believed to rise. (Read the story of the "Seven Year Famine.")

Herodotus, the Greek historian, described the Season of Inundation when the river Nile flooded:

> "All of Egypt becomes a sea. Only the towns remain above water, looking rather like islands in the Aegean. Shipping no longer follows the stream but goes straight across the country. When the waters recede they leave behind a layer of fertile silt "Black Land," distinct from sterile "Red Land" of the surrounding desert."

Dwellings were built either on land rising at the edge of the flood plain or on mounds of accumulated rubble from buildings destroyed by previous floods. People moved between their "island" dwellings by boat. Dikes were built around villages to keep back the floodwaters.

1 cubit =	45 cm	
1 cubit =	⌐	
1 palm =	⌒	
7 palms	=	1 ⌐
/	=	1
//	=	2, etc.
⌒	=	10

It is harvest time in the village. It will be New Year soon and the floodwaters will arrive.
The houses are built on high ground to avoid flooding.

Imagine the village during the flood. Draw a picture on a separate piece of paper.

Scribes recorded the rising waters on nilometers each year. This helped them
predict the final flood levels so they could forewarn the people of possible
disaster. It also helped them estimate the tax on crops in the coming year.
Below is a record of nilometer readings taken over seven years showing the
highest point of the flood each year.

> "12 cubits bring famine, 14 rejoicing, 16 security
> and 18 luxury. A rise of 16 cubits is just right."

They are marked off in cubits 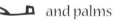 and palms .

(7 palms = 1 cubit) 1 cubit is approximately 45 cm.

Work out the approximate length of 1 palm . _____

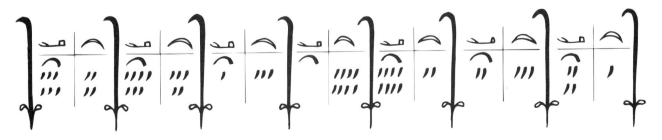

Use the information above to make a block graph. Color the good years green and the bad years red.

Teachers Notes

The picture on the next page, taken from a tomb painting, illustrates the sequence of the harvest, starting from the bottom left to right and top right to left. Students will need page 39 to complete page 41.

Vocabulary: reap   sickle   pannier   kernels   win   now   chaff

Extension

1. Imagine you are a peasant. You feel your tax demand is too high and you can not afford to pay it. Present a case to the tax inspector, explaining why you think your tax is unfair.

The scene shows harvesters working to the rhythm of harvest songs and using wooden sickles set with flint blades. They cut just the heads of grain and left the straw to be collected later for brickmaking, basket weaving and fueling pottery kilns.

Note the peasants resting under a tree, one is playing a flute. Little girls squabble over the gleanings and a disabled person leans on his crutch. The grain is being carried off in panniers to the threshing floor, where it is raked out and trampled by oxen, driven around and around.

Winnowers with heads covered from sun and dust use wooden bats to throw the grain into the air. The breeze blows away the chaff.

During the growing season the tax inspector called to assess the tax, which was set at around 20% of the expected crop yield, depending on the quality of land and anticipated flood levels, which were determined by nilometer readings (see page 36-37, The Flood). Pests like mice or plagues of locusts, even hippopotamuses, could ruin a farmer's crop. Tomb paintings often show prostrate defaulters being beaten by the tax collector's henchmen.

Consider the peasants' woes:

> "Mice abound in the fields, locusts descend and animals eat the crop. What remains is taken by thieves. The hire of oxen is wasted because the animals have died. Then the scribe arrives at the riverbank to register the tax on the harvest."

At harvest time granary barges were moored alongside the fields. Grain was collected and transported to the temple or state granaries to be distributed later by smaller cargo boats as payment to employees (see pages 108–109, Measures).

This scene comes from the tomb of Menna of Thebes. Menna, the landowner, oversees the harvesters from his kiosk. The grain must be harvested and taken to the granary before the river floods in the New Year.

△ **Color and discuss what is happening in the tomb painting.**

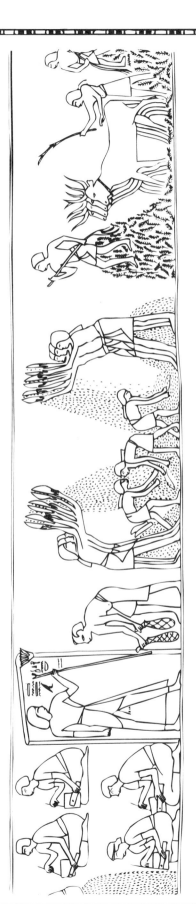

See page 38 for Harvest Time background information and teachers notes.

Look at the harvest scene then draw a picture in each of the boxes below.

1. Reaping wheat with sickles.	2. Carrying wheat in panniers.
3. Raking out sheaves of wheat.	4. Oxen treading wheat kernels.
5. Peasants winnowing chaff from grain.	6. Scribes recording quantities.

Teachers Notes

The cloze comprehension describes how the calendar was invented and explains the basis for the Egyptians' ten-day week. Why do you think it was important for the ancient Egyptians to have an accurate calendar?

Cloze passage answers:

years, astronomy, sky, horizon, star, dawn, rise, New Year, months, gods, days, seasons

Extension

1. Compare the table for the Egyptian calendar with a similar table for the calendar we use.

The calendar was one of the Egyptians' greatest inventions. It was later adapted by the Romans, who adopted a seven-day week. Farmers needed to organize their activities in accordance with the seasons and so the calendar was designed by temple astronomers, known as "Keepers of the Time," who observed the night sky and could describe the changes throughout the year. The appearance of Sirius, the Dog Star, was of particular importance to the farmer, for it signaled the arrival of the flood.

Use these words to complete the passage.

dawn	horizon
sky	months
rise	New Year
days	seasons
years	gods
star	astronomy

The calendar we use is based on the one the ancient Egyptians invented more than 5,000

_____ ago.

Some priests studied _____ . They watched the movement of the stars

across the _____ at night. A different set of stars appeared at dawn on the eastern

_____ every ten days. From this came their ten-day week.

Every three hundred and sixty-five days Sirius, the brightest _____ , appeared on the horizon at

_____ . The Nile waters began to _____ at the same time. This was so important

to the Egyptians, they celebrated the event as their _____ _____ .

The Egyptians divided the year into twelve equal _____ . They added on an extra five

days for birthdays of _____ and goddesses. Altogether this made up the 365 _____

of the year.

The months were divided equally into three _____ – Akhet, Peret and Shemu.

Use the information above to help you complete a table for the Egyptian calendar.

_____ days = 1 week		_____ seasons = 1 year
_____ days = 1 year		_____ months = 1 season
_____ weeks = 1 year		_____ days = 1 month
_____ months = 1 year		_____ weeks = 1 month

Teachers Notes

Reflecting on the design of the dwelling and observing activities around the farmhouse can help in imagining everyday rural life. Consider how the house is suited to the climate and way of life (see pages 58–59 and 60–61 for comparisons with town and village life).

Extension

1. Design your own farmhouse similar to the one in the picture.

2. Draw a plan. Include a scale and list of building materials.

Dwellings were designed to give relief from the dazzling light and scorching sun outdoors. The cool inner shade of the dark rooms was lit by small, high windows, often shaded with reed blinds.

Mud brick was the most common building material. Woven reed panels covered the roof timbers and were reinforced with mud plaster. Walls inside and out were often whitewashed and sometimes decorated with colored patterns.

Outside, a flight of mud brick steps led to a flat roof with vents to the rooms below. They were directed for catching the breeze constantly blowing from the north. A parapet wall around the flat roof made a safe extension to a family's living space. An awning of woven reeds gave shade for sedentary activities like spinning and weaving. A walled courtyard provided some protection from winter sandstorms and prowling animals in the night.

Household grain was stored in mud-brick silos that were filled from the top by climbing a ladder. Grinding corn on a stone quern to make flour was a daily chore. Fetching water was another daily chore. Porous earthenware jars kept water cool.

Cattle needed good grazing pastures, so only wealthy farmers could afford to keep large herds. Goats and sheep were more common as they grazed on shrub land. Women made butter and cheese from the animals' milk.

Children did many useful tasks: they scared off pigeons and sparrows from freshly seeded land, chased goats and sheep down to the water's edge to drink and collected eggs from the nests of ducks and geese.

Farmhouses were made of mud bricks and then plastered and whitewashed. Bundles of reeds were used for the pillars and trunks of palm trees for the roof timbers.

Look at the picture of the farmhouse. Describe the activities going on around the house.

_____

_____

_____

_____

On a separate piece of paper, make a list of the main features and draw a plan of the house above.

Soul House

Peasant farmers lived in far humbler dwellings like this small, model clay house found in a tomb.

Make a model soul house from clay.

Teachers Notes

The pictures convey the Egyptians' expertise in breeding and training animals. Completing the picture of the wall painting demonstrates the archaeologist's task of reconstructing artifacts.

Extension

1. What pets do students have? Find out which countries they originate from.

2. What animals do farmers keep?

The fertile valley supported a great variety of animals. Scrub land around the watercourses in desert valleys was home to even more.

Cattle were trained to pull plows and tread corn around the threshing floor. The donkey was first domesticated in Egypt and used as a beast of burden. Oxen were used as draft animals for shifting heavy loads.

Every year huge, flocks of migrating wildfowl passed through the valley. Cranes, ducks and geese were trapped in nets and then fattened with grain for their meat. Pelicans were also caught and kept in captivity for their eggs.

The Egyptians were the first to domesticate the cat – the large wild cat of the marshlands. It was trained to retrieve wildfowl that had been felled by the master's throwing stick from the reeds.

Many households had a pet baboon, which are shown in paintings helping pick figs.

Pigs are depicted being driven over the ground to tread in freshly scattered grain.

Egyptians had always been keen hunters and observers of animal behavior. They attempted to domesticate all kinds of species. Many animals can be tamed but do not always breed in captivity. Egyptians tried but failed to domesticate gazelles and hyenas, which presumably they wanted for meat. However, they were the first people to domesticate honeybees and they also succeeded in taming cheetahs to run alongside the nobleman's horse and chariot on hunting expeditions across the desert. Dogs were trained to follow the chase and hunt in packs, and were also used as sniffer dogs.

Animals were very much part of life in Egypt. The first farmers not only cultivated wild plants they also domesticated wild animals.

Tomb paintings show herdsmen with all kinds of animals. Goats, sheep, pigs and cattle were kept for their meat but Egyptians also found animals useful in other ways.

Describe what is happening in these pictures.

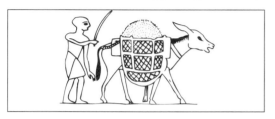

_____

_____

_____

_____

_____

_____

_____

_____

_____

_____

_____

_____

Here is a copy of a damaged wall painting. Complete the picture to see how the pigs are helping the farmer.

Teachers Notes

This exercise requires identifying the source of different foods and sorting them into groups. It is also an opportunity to reflect on our own diet.

Extension

1. Which of the foods listed have you never eaten? What fruit and vegetables do you eat that are not on the list?

2. Find out about the Egyptians' staple food and how it was made.

3. Look at pictures of tomb paintings where there are offering tables piled with food. What foods can you recognize?

4. Sample some typically Egyptian foods or prepare a simple Egyptian meal.

Egyptians had a mainly vegetarian diet. They all ate a lot of bread, which, together with beer, was their staple diet. The Greeks called them the "bread eaters." A soldier's bread ration was 4 to 5 pounds per day (2.5 kg)! There were many varieties. Some were like cakes, sweetened with dates or honey. A weak but nutritious beer was made from crumbled barley bread that had been left to ferment. It was drunk through straws with filters for holding back the heavy sediment.

Beef was a rare treat except for the wealthy, who regularly feasted at banquets on every kind of luxury. Most people received their protein from legumes. This was occasionally supplemented with dairy products, wild game, fish, goat, mutton, or pork. Villages kept pigs that thrived on human waste and, judging from the quantities of bones archaeologists have found in village garbage, pork was eaten regularly, even though it was declared unclean by the priests.

Figs and dates were dried and stored for eating throughout the year. Grapes needed constant tending in vineyards, so only the wealthy could afford to drink wine made from grapes. Date and pomegranate wines were more commonly drunk.

Linseed, sesame and castor oils were used for cooking, which was usually done over an open courtyard fire fueled with dry animal dung. A mud-brick oven was used for baking bread.

Weddings, funeral ceremonies and festivals were times of feasting. A funeral feast of a nobleman was recorded to include barley bread, fish, pigeon stew, roast quail, leg of beef, stewed figs, cheese, honeycakes and wine.

Here are some of the things Egyptians ate. Number the pictures accordingly to the labels then draw and complete the table below on a separate piece of paper.

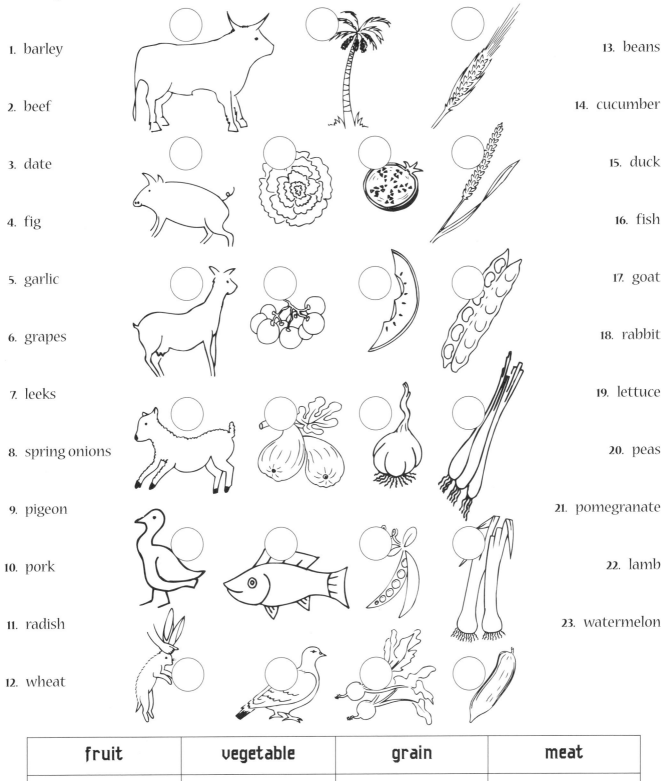

1. barley

2. beef

3. date

4. fig

5. garlic

6. grapes

7. leeks

8. spring onions

9. pigeon

10. pork

11. radish

12. wheat

13. beans

14. cucumber

15. duck

16. fish

17. goat

18. rabbit

19. lettuce

20. peas

21. pomegranate

22. lamb

23. watermelon

fruit	vegetable	grain	meat

Teachers Notes

Examples are used to demonstrate the Egyptians' sophisticated system of bartering.

Extension

Design and make a balance scale with a set of weights suitable for weighing precious gemstones. Balance scales with weights, often made in the shape of a series of animal heads, were used for weighing out goods. Precious metals and gemstones were weighed in small units called "kites." There were ten kites to a "deben." If a deben weighed 100 grams, how many grams did a kite weigh?

To make the scale you will need: thin dowel, cotton, foil plates and modeling clay for making weights. Collect sets of "gem" stones for weighing.

All goods had an agreed value based on the weight of copper. With foreigners, if values had not been established through an ongoing trading relationship, a system of silent bartering operated. Goods were gradually laid out until an acceptable offer was made. Hatshepsut's trading expedition to Punt for frankincense and myrrh proceeded in this way.

Egyptians bartered in the market instead of using money. They worked out the value of something by reckoning its value in the weight of copper. One deben of copper weighed 100 grams.

 A farmer wants to barter some of his goats for a donkey. How many goats did he have to give for the donkey if the donkey is reckoned to be worth 50 debens of copper and his goats, 10 debens of copper each?

He will have to give _____ goats for the donkey.

Here are some things valued in debens of copper.

Debens			Debens			Debens		
2		figs	6		leather skin	15		sheet
3		loincloth	7		goose	18		bed
4		Nile perch	8		sack of barley	20		bronze vase
5		jar of honey	10		goat	50		donkey
6		collar of beads	12		leg of ox	100		ox

You could barter a bronze vase, worth 20 debens, for all of these items:

6   +   6   +   4   +   4   =   20 debens

 Find the value of these items in debens. On a separate piece of paper draw the things you could barter them for.

a.   b.   c.   d.

   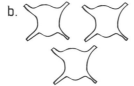   

_____   _____   _____   _____

Teachers Notes

The conventions and grid system used by the Egyptian artist are followed.

Vocabulary: proportion   profile   grid

Extension

1. Make a wall collage titled "Men and Women Returning from Market."

   Look at photographs of tomb paintings and observe conventions including color combinations and skin color. Note the skin tone of men is darker than women's and outlines of paintings are usually marked in red first.

   Enlarge the sketch, making the figures 2 – 3 times the size.

   For the collage, use black yarn (hair), white tissue (translucent clothing), gold paper (jewelry) and shiny paper (market produce).

   Cut out the figures and arrange in two panels, one of men and one of women. Use a repeat decorative border made from strips of paper or simple block printing, as found in pictures of tomb paintings.

   Note: Eyes are shown face-on in heavy black outline with the face in profile.
            Shoulders and torso are shown from the front and the remainder of the body in profile.

Peasant women took freshly baked bread, jugs of beer and surplus produce from the household vegetable plot, such as bunches of onions, lettuces, peas, or beans to market. They also took lengths of homespun, coarsely-woven cloth. Local craftsmen laid out jewelry, sandals, carved shrine figures, clay cooking pots, woven mats, baskets and stools.

Egyptian artists followed strict rules for the position and proportions of different parts of the body. A grid was used to transfer and enlarge a drawing onto a wall.

Take up an Egyptian pose. Which parts of your body are in profile and which parts are face on?

Profile _____

Face on _____

Look at the drawing below and, counting the number of squares, complete the list of proportions. The first one is done for you.

head	_3 x 3_
head to toe	_____
shoulder to waist	_____
shoulder to fingertips	_____
width of shoulders	_____
elbow to fingertips	_____
waist to knee	_____
knee to foot	_____
toe to heel	_____

Look carefully at the picture and follow these rules to help you draw a person carrying goods from market. You will need some large grid paper.

Teachers Notes

This activity illustrates how the levels in Egyptian society were drawn and considers the relative status attributed to different occupations.

Extension

1. Imagine the life of a goldminer in the desert. Much of Egypt's wealth came from gold mined in the scorching heat of the Eastern Desert. Criminals, prisoners of war and slaves were used as gold-miners. Water was rationed.

Professional people first trained as scribes, which in itself bestowed a position of privilege above that of manual workers and confirmed loyalty to the ruling class. A scribe's training was arduous. Many years were spent laboriously copying out hieroglyphic texts extolling the virtues of being a scribe:

> "Be a scribe! It saves you from hard work and
> preserves you from every kind of labor."

It also encouraged an attitude of superiority towards the lower classes:

> "The potter is buried in earth while he is still among the living.
> He grubs about in the mud more than any pig…"

As a scribe, it was possible to rise to eminence as an officer of state, although these positions were usually hereditary. Further training for a professional occupation was a more realistic aspiration. Many scribes trained to become architects, surveyors and engineers – the professional people needed for the extensive building projects undertaken by the state.

Officers of state often had elaborate titles, such as "Master of the Secrets of the Royal Decrees" and "Master of Largesse," who was responsible for distributing gifts as rewards to favored officials and governors, and ensuring the needy did not starve during times of hardship. "Overseer of the Granaries" was a key position, for the granaries were the "banks" of Egypt, with responsibility for huge stocks of grain, enough at times to feed the nation for a year or more. Laborers and craftsmen received regular payments in grain so large consignments were continually being moved from the granaries, which all had to be recorded by teams of scribes.

Viziers were the power behind the throne. Second only to the king, they were able to carry out the affairs of the state in the king's absence. Upper and Lower Egypt usually had separate bureaucracies so there were two Viziers, one based in Thebes, the other in Memphis. Overseers, with their different responsibilities, were accountable to the respective Vizier.

By the Middle Kingdom, noblemen and their families were becoming extremely wealthy and powerful, living a life of unimaginable luxury. They accumulated their fortune from local taxes paid by peasants and craftsmen, as well as rent from estates and tributes from the king, who needed their allegiance. They also owned workshops and had farms with large herds of valuable cattle. They lived in magnificent country homes set in idyllic gardens with ornamental pools. Dancers and musicians frequently entertained at the many banquets. Skilled craftsmen, working with exotic woods and gold, produced all manner of finery to satisfy the desires of the ruling class.

Egyptian children usually followed in their parents' footsteps, learning their trade from their parents. However, a son of a poor peasant farmer who showed great talent could go to a temple school and train to be a scribe. This could open the door to many professions. Scribes had a high opinion of themselves and were very aware of their position in society.

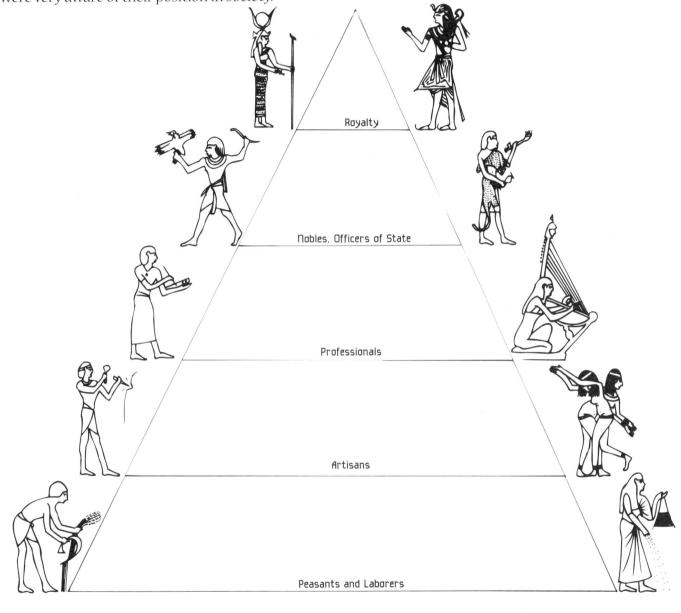

Look at the pyramid showing the different levels in Egyptian society. Sort and write the occupations below on the pyramid according to which you think Egyptians thought were most important.

sculptor	scribe	servant	sailor	engineer	high priest	water carrier
governor	soldier	laborer	potter	ferryman	quarryman	farmworker
architect	vizier	musician	priest	goldsmith	landowner	tax collector
carpenter	queen	surveyor	doctor	embalmer	fisherman	army general
painter	king	overseer	dancer	goldminer		

Teachers Notes

The various titles of the king refer to his divine power and immortality and also as a unifier of the Two Lands – Upper and Lower Egypt.

Vocabulary: pharaoh   unite   symbol   reincarnation   eternal   divine

Picture and label matches:

Mighty Bull, He Who Unites The Two Lands, Horus The Falcon, Two Ladies, He Of The Sedge And The Bee

Extension

1. Look for pictures of kings to find out about their costumes and the different crowns they wore. Draw and label a picture of a king.

2. Find out about the Heb Sed Festival. Every 30 years there was a jubilee when the king had to run around a course set out by markers, proving he was still fit to reign.

3. Find out about Hatshepsut, the one and only female pharaoh. Hatshepsut took the unusual stance of becoming a pharaoh. She adopted the king's regalia, having dispensed with the queen's. She even took to wearing the regal beard (see pages 18–21, Foreign Trade and pages 116–119, Timeline).

The king was crowned with the words "You arise a god." He was regarded as the son of Ra the Sun god, and embodiment of the sky god, Horus the Falcon. When he died he became Osiris, God of the Underworld. The successor at his coronation was, in turn, proclaimed the reincarnation of Horus the Falcon, the eternal king (see pages 64–71, Religion section and pages 78–79, Osiris, God of the Underworld).

The king's divine powers brought order and harmony to Egypt. He controlled the river and made the crops grow. He protected his people and brought them good fortune. He was depicted as a towering figure, wielding a mattock for cutting an irrigation canal, or striking his enemies and treading them under foot.

He lived apart from ordinary mortals. Every aspect of his life was an elaborate ritual. He wore the costume of kings. His crowns, described as "great of magic," had their own divine power. The crown with tall feathers identified him as a god. As a warrior pharaoh, leading his troops to battle, he wore the Blue Crown or Crown of Victory (see Background History – page 3).

Typically attired, a king wore the double crown - the red crown of Lower Egypt and the white crown of Upper Egypt, a false braided beard, the tail of a bull or a giraffe, a beaded apron and, like the god Osiris, carried the crook and flail, symbols of the shepherd and the harvester.

Pharaoh means great house or palace. It was only in later years the king was known as Pharaoh, the one who lived in the great house.

The king had many titles. Some are listed below.

Horus The Falcon   He Of The Sedge And The Bee   Mighty Bull
Two Ladies   He Who Unites The Two Lands

 Use the above to fill in the missing information below. Match the pictures to the titles and label each one.

Egyptians believed their king had superhuman powers. He made the Nile flood and the plants grow. He protected his people from enemies with the strength of a

_____.

The first king of Egypt was Menes. He wore the double crown, the white crown of Upper Egypt in the south and the red crown of Lower Egypt in the north. The crown symbolized the title

_____.

Whenever a new king was crowned he became the reincarnation of the eternal sky god who swept across the heavens looking down upon his kingdom. He was

_____.

Upon his brow the king wore the vulture goddess, Nekhbet of Upper Egypt and the cobra goddess, Wadjyt of Lower Egypt. They gave him divine protection and the title

_____.

was another of the king's titles. The sedge was a symbol of Upper Egypt and the bee of Lower Egypt.

 On a separate piece of paper draw three symbols for Upper Egypt and three for Lower Egypt.

Teachers Notes

Lifting the flaps of the model reveals daily life in the house of an official where many servants are at work. Students will need a copy of the bottom of this page, as well as a copy of page 59 to complete this activity.

Basement – Servants are spinning, weaving, grinding and sieving corn.

First Floor – Servants are carrying food and flowers to the master, who is seated upon a dais in the main room.

Top Floor – Attendants are fanning the chief scribe, who is waiting to inspect the contents of the storehouse.

Servants are carrying supplies up the staircase to a canopied kitchen area on the roof. Grain silos are also located here.

Cut out around the inside and outside of the house.

Cut along the dotted lines.

Staple the corners of the outside onto the inside of the house.

Lift each flap to see what is happening in each room.

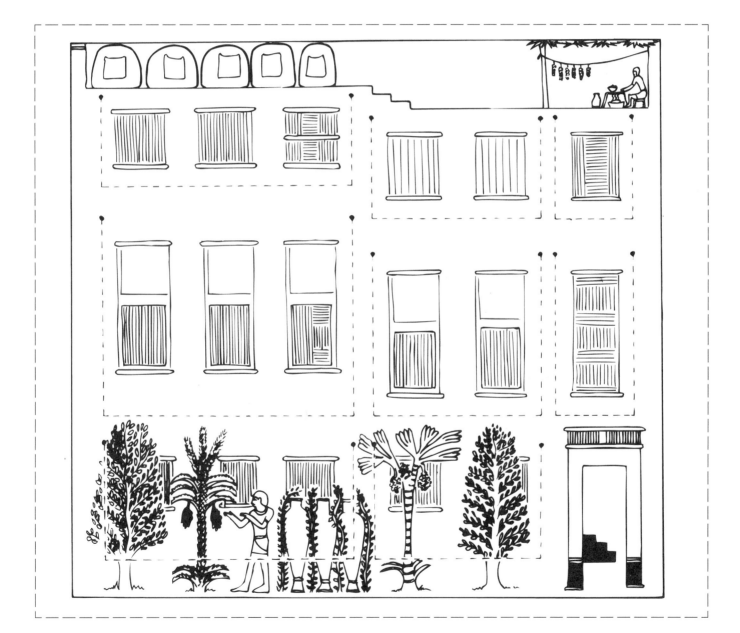

Teachers Notes

The plan shows the closely contained walled village of Deir el-Medina, located in the hills of the Western Desert and occupied by the craftsmen who worked in the Valley of the Kings. The house illustrated can be located on the plan – fifth down on the right.

Extension

1. Locate Deir el-Medina on a map (see page 11).

2. The simple furnishings would have included: beds with headrests, storage chests and baskets, tables, pot stands, stools, storage jars, cooking pots and shrine figures. Look for pictures of some of these things and draw or make models of some.

3. The first strike ever recorded was made by residents of Deir el-Medina. Write a letter to be handed in at the temple explaining why the workers downed tools and on what terms they are prepared to return to work.

   As the Empire declined and corruption became rife, food deliveries to the village were often delayed. One day, around 1170 B.C., the work gangs downed tools and marched to the temple of Rameses II chanting "We are hungry! We are hungry!" Food deliveries had been delayed for two months. The strike continued for eight days, until the two months outstanding had been paid in full.

4. Write a story – "The Tomb Robbers."

Most mud-brick buildings were swept away by the river long ago but, set back in the desert well above the flood plain, the remains of Deir el-Medina provide valuable evidence of village life in ancient Egypt.

It was a village of unusually literate and well-paid craftsmen. Remotely situated in the barren desert, there was little opportunity for growing vegetables or keeping animals, other than pigs. The villagers were dependent on a regular delivery of supplies. All their water had to be carried up from the valley on the back of donkeys.

The menfolk were often away for nine days at a time, working in the royal tombs at a secret location in a desert valley some miles distant. In spite of high security, however, the tombs were frequently broken into and looted. During times of food shortage people turned more and more to robbing tombs and selling the loot for grain.

Deir el-Medina was a village occupied by craftsmen and their families for 500 years. It was situated in the sun-scorched hills across the river from Thebes. The craftsmen were employed to build tombs in the Valley of the Kings.

Here is a picture of one of their houses and a plan of the village.

 Identify the house on the plan. Shade it red.

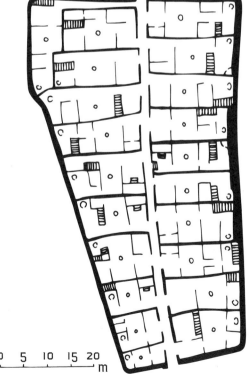

Label the following features of the house:

1. front door
2. entrance room with steps up to chapel
3. main living room
4. central pillar
5. bedroom
6. walled courtyard
7. stairs leading to rooftop
8. shaded kitchen area
9. brick oven
10. storage cellars

 Which of these houses would you choose? Shade it blue.
Draw an enlarged plan (x 5) of your house.
Label the features from above on your plan.

0 5 10 15 20
m

Teachers Notes

The work of archaeologists in piecing together life in ancient Egypt can be appreciated by carefully studying the drawings of artisans and laborers based on primary sources.

Extension

1. Investigate the work of different craftsmen. Search in books for photographs of anything that could provide clues. Look carefully at wall paintings and study some of the things craftsmen made (see pages 90–99, Jewelry section).

Egypt's dry climate and desert sands have immaculately preserved many intricately decorated panels found on tomb and temple walls, illustrating everyday life in ancient Egypt. Together with explanatory hieroglyphs, these paintings have provided archaeologists with unparalleled evidence about life in ancient Egypt.

The wall paintings are from the tomb of Rekhmire, a vizier of Upper Egypt, and are part of a series depicting all the activities of people under his jurisdiction. Rekhmire takes the credit for their work.

> "Making furniture in ivory and ebony...in real cedar from the heights of the terraced hills, by this official who establishes guidelines and controls the hands of the craftsmen."

Egyptians built their temples and tombs to last forever. They are full of clues which give us a good idea about the way of life in ancient Egypt.

△ **Study the pictures taken from wall paintings in Egyptian tombs showing laborers and craftsmen at work.**

△ **Describe how ancient Egyptians made sun-dried bricks from mud and straw using a wooden box mold.**

_____

_____

_____

△ **On a separate piece of paper draw and label the following carpenter's tools and examples of their work: adze (axe/chisel), saw, bow-drill, storage box, bed frame and lotus bud column.**

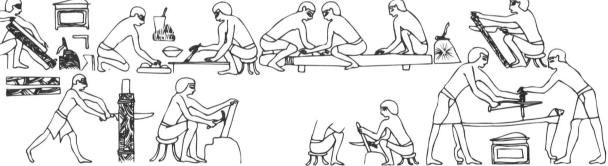

△ **Label the following: 1. piles of charcoal, 2. stoking the furnace, 3. working foot bellows, 4. lifting a crucible with bent branches, 5. bringing ingots and baskets of ore, 6. filling the mold with molten metal and 7. cast bronze doors.**

Teachers Notes

The flip book introduces some of the most popular animal gods.

Extension

1. Read the myth of Horus avenging the death of his father, Osiris. After an eighty-year battle against his cruel uncle Seth, the murderous brother of Osiris, Horus eventually claimed the throne of Egypt, which was his rightful inheritance. Thereafter the "Horus Throne" was handed to a human successor, who became the reincarnation of Horus (see pages 56–57, Kings; 92–93, Amulets – Eye of Horus; 78–79, Osiris, God of the Underworld).

2. Look for pictures of Seth, the mysterious, donkey-like animal god of chaos and evil, who ruled the deserts and brought the storms. Make a picture of your own mysterious animal god.

3. Find out about the household gods, Bes and Taweret. Make a model or picture of one of them.

4. Find out about the Apis bull and the cat goddess, Bastet.

Egyptians revered many of the animals that lived in the valley and along the desert fringe. They believed these animals had divine powers and admired them for their special qualities, like the tender care of a cow for her calves. They even admired animals they feared, the crocodile for its strength and the lion for its fierceness. They imagined certain animals embodied particular gods and goddesses. These were sacred and worshipped at cult centers. Priests, wearing animal masks, gave voice to these gods and made their wishes known – according to the priests' interpretations. Many deities came to have a human body with the head of an animal. Notice the gods carried in their left hands the ankh, which was the sacred symbol of life, and in their right hand the divine scepter, which all gods and kings carried.

1. Horus appears throughout Egyptian mythology in varying forms. As a sky god he was often portrayed as a winged sun-disc above a sacred doorway. As Horus, son of Isis, seated on his mother's lap with a finger in his mouth, he reminds us of baby Jesus. It is an image similar to, but pre-dating, the Virgin Mary with Child.

2. Sobek, the crocodile god, constantly needed placating, especially along stretches of crocodile-infested waters. At Crocodilopolis in the Faiyum Oasis, jewel-studded crocodiles lolled in temple pools and mummified crocodiles were buried in the necropolis.

3. Thoth was the god of wisdom and writing. He was the patron of scribes and was also associated with the moon. He caused moonlight to brighten the night sky and dispel the fearful darkness.

4. Anubis, god of the Dead, led away the dead person's soul (see pages 70–71).

5. Khnum was known as the "Potter God." He created all living creatures from clay on his divine potter's wheel. Eventually tiring of his work, he placed a potter's wheel in the womb of every female creature. He then had only to breathe life into each new being.

6. Bes, the protector of the family, who brought health and happiness, was a grotesque, bandy-legged dwarf god with the mane and ears of a lion and a protruding tongue.

7. Taweret, the goddess who protected women and children, had the head and body of a pregnant hippopotamus, with the arms and legs of a lion and the back and tail of a crocodile.

8. The Apis bull personified the god Ptah, the patron of craftsmen, and resided in Ptah's temple at Memphis. It had special white markings on its forehead and chest. When it died, it was mummified and buried with great ceremony. A successor with identical markings then had to be found.

9. The much-loved domestic cat was worshipped as Bastet, goddess of joy and love, and was represented as a woman with a cat's head. When a cat died the family mourned. They shaved off their eyebrows and even took their embalmed pet to the temple at Bubastis for burial. During excavations of the Suez Canal, tons of mummified cats were dug up from the site of an ancient necropolis and exported as fertilizer.

cardboard

Many Egyptian gods had a human body with the head of an animal.

Color and cut out the pictures to make a flip book of animal gods. Label each one.

- Horus — falcon god of the sky
- Sobek — crocodile god of water
- Thoth — ibis god of wisdom and writing
- Anubis — jackal god of the dead
- Khnum — ram god, the giver of life

Teachers Notes

The pictures can be rearranged like a storyboard, telling the story of Ra's daily journey across the sky and describing the cycle of day and night.

Extension

Select one part of the story of Ra and write a news report detailing all aspects of the event.

> *"Praise to you who rise in gold and illumine the*
> *Two Lands by day at your birth."*
> Prayer to the Sun

When Egyptians saw eggs hatching from the scarab beetle's ball of dung they were reminded of how life magically recreates itself, the scarab became a symbol of resurrection. As a hieroglyph, it meant "to come into existence," just like the Sun, which they imagined was reborn each day.

The daily cycle of the Sun is particularly apparent in Egypt. At dawn the Sun appears above the hills of the Eastern Desert, during the course of the day, it arches over the river valley and in the evening sets in the west. Egyptians thought of the Sun as light shining from Ra's eye. Watching it slip below the horizon of the Western Desert, they imagined Ra dying and descending into the Underworld. This is why corpses were always buried in the Western Desert and why it was known as the "Land of the Dead." As Ra passed into the Underworld of Osiris, Egyptians imagined his radiant light awakening the dead souls, or "Westerners" as they were called.

The dawn was always greeted with joy, for each day was a hard-won victory over the powers of darkness. If Ra was ever to lose the battle against the demons of the Underworld, the Sun would not rise and the waters of chaos would cover the Earth.

Ra was not alone on his journey. He was protected by a long, coiled serpent. His boat was guided by pilot fish and dragged through the night sky by jackals and crowned cobras. The gods were at his side; Thoth set the course, Horus steered the boat and Seth stood at the prow, warding off the powers of darkness. The king, who was the son of Ra, ensured the everlasting cycle of day and night by his constant devotion.

During the Old Kingdom the dead king was provided with a funerary boat (buried in a pit next to his pyramid) so he could join Ra on his journey across the sky.

Of all the gods, Egyptians believed Ra the Sun god was the most important, for he created the world.

 **Read the passages below. Color, cut out and rearrange the pictures telling the story of Ra.
Glue on a separate piece of paper and write a suitable caption for each picture.**

The lions of the desert horizons guarded Ra as he rose above the hills in the east each morning and sank below the hills in the west at night.

Every day at dawn baboons sat waiting for the first rays of daylight. They greeted the Sun with joyful dancing.

Egyptians had a special name for the rising Sun. They called it Khepri, which was their name for the scarab beetle that pushed along its eggs inside a ball of dung. Egyptians imagined Khepri pushing the Sun up into the sky just like the beetle. Every morning Khepri stepped aboard the "Day Boat" to sail across the sky towards the West.

By midday the Sun was overhead and blazing down. It had become "Ra and Horus of the Two Horizons." This was the strong, young Sun god, with the head of a hawk.

By evening, the Sun was dying and sinking below the western horizon. It was now the ancient ram-headed god, Ra Atum. He boarded the night boat and began the dangerous journey across the sky of the Underworld beneath the Earth.

Apophis, the most terrible of fiends, was lying in wait. Ra Atum, disguised as a cat, chopped off his head with a knife, but every night Apophis returned.

Teachers Notes

A family tree can be constructed from the information given. The myth of Nut introduces another explanation for the daily cycle of the Sun.

Extension

1. Look for pictures of ceilings in tombs depicting Nut as the night sky. Make a star print block and use it to print gold stars on a deep blue background. Cut out the shape of Nut's outstretched body and fix to the ceiling to represent the Egyptian night sky.

Egyptians imagined the sky was the goddess Nut, stretching her star-spangled body over the Earth. Every evening she swallowed the Sun. During the night it passed through her body and was reborn each morning. Nut also gave birth to the stars and the planets, which were placed on her belly.

Seth, God of Evil and Lord of Upper Egypt, was associated with the desert and storms. He was represented by a big-eared mythical beast that resembled a donkey or an anteater.

Read the story of the Ennaed then label the picture.

Ra-Atum and his divine family were known and worshipped as the Great Ennaed of Heliopolis.

The Sun God, Ra-Atum, made all of creation out of himself. From his spittle came Tefnut, Goddess of Moisture, and from his breath came Shu, God of Air.

Tefnut and Shu had twins, Nut the Sky Goddess and Geb the Earth God. They loved one another but their father was jealous and tore them apart. He trampled Geb beneath his feet and raised Nut high up into the sky. Then he put a curse on Nut so she could never give birth. But Nut challenged Thoth, God of Time, to a game of checkers and won five days from him to add to the 360 days of the year. She could then give birth since these days did not fall under her father's curse.

Nut and Geb were married and had five children. On the first day Osiris, God of the Underworld, was born, on the second, Horus the Elder, on the third Seth, God of Evil, on the fourth Isis, Mother Goddess and on the fifth a daughter, Nepthys.

 Draw a family tree of the Great Ennaed on a separate piece of paper.

 Who's who?

1. Who was Geb's father? _____

2. Who was Nut's mother? _____

3. Who was Seth's father? _____

4. Who was Osiris' mother? _____

5. Who were Ra-Atum's grandchildren? _____

   _____

6. Who were Ra-Atum's great grandchildren? _____

   _____

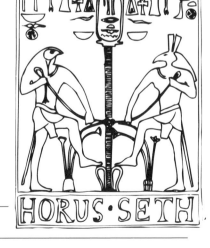

Teachers Notes

An animal mask, using simple paper sculpture, is made by cutting and folding a single sheet of paper and decorating with cut paper shapes.

Extension

Adapt the Anubis mask to make the heads of other animal gods (see pages 64-56, Animal Gods).

Priests who carried out embalming and funeral ceremonies impersonated Anubis by wearing a jackal-headed mask.

Jackals are scavengers and have always been associated with the dead. At night they prowled around ancient cemeteries along the desert edge, digging up human bones. The earliest graves were covered in heavy stones to protect the dead from marauding jackals. If a body was eaten there was no chance of an afterlife (see pages 72–73, Mummies). By elevating the jackal to god of the dead, Egyptians felt they could appease his nature. They revered the jackal as "Lord of the Necropolis."

Ancient myth tells how Anubis created the first mummy. He helped Isis wrap her dead husband, Osiris, in bandages. Known as "He who belongs to the mummy wrappings," Anubis became the patron of embalmers and presided over the burial rites. He led the dead soul to the afterlife and supervised the "Weighing of the Heart in the Hall of Judgment" (see pages 76–77, Weighing of the Heart).

Anubis was always black, like mummified corpses and the fertile silt from which new growth sprouted each year. Black became the color representing rebirth.

Anubis was the god of the dead. A priest wore the mask of Anubis during the burial ceremony.

 To make an Anubis mask you will need:

- thin black cardboard
- colored paper
- gold paper
- tape
- hat elastic
- glue
- thin cardboard for template

1. Make the template below scaled up two times (1:2). Cut out from black cardboard.
2. Bend as shown and fasten with tape and glue.
3. Decorate the eyes and ears with gold paper.
4. Cut the colored paper as shown and fix to the mask.

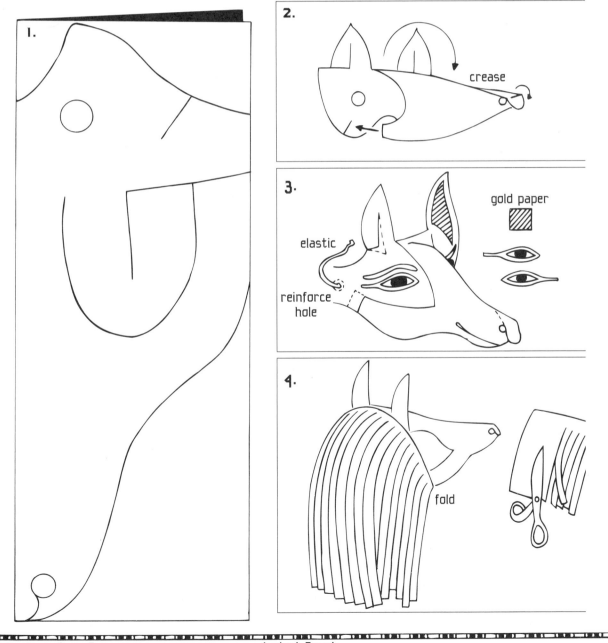

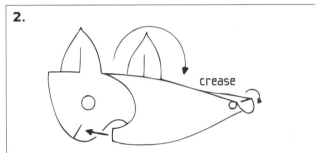

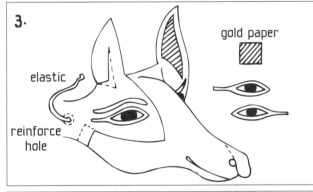

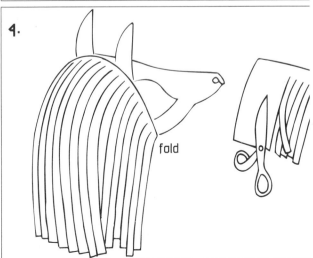

Teachers Notes

The mummy bookmark, labeled on the back, introduces some common symbols and characters associated with the dead.

Extension

1. Find out about the work of embalmers.

2. Make either a miniature or life-size mummy. Use bound rolled newspaper for the body and wrap in strips of sheeting decorated with amulets. Include a heart scarab for protecting the dead soul during the Weighing of the Heart ceremony (see pages 92–93, Amulets).

3. Make an enlarged picture of the mummy case using a photocopier.

4. Make a life-sized mummy case using chicken wire and papier-mâché. Paint and decorate with symbols cut from paper. Seal with a varnish of glue.

5. Make a set of Canopic jars from clay. Human-headed Imsety guarded the liver, baboon-headed Hapy, the lungs, jack-headed Duamutef, the stomach and falcon-headed Qebehsenuef, the intestines.

The word "mummy" is derived from the Arabic word for bitumen, which was incorrectly thought to be the substance used for embalming dead bodies.

The mummy case was formed from cartonnage, a material made from layers of linen or papyrus stiffened with plaster. The case was usually decorated inside and out. Often the mummy was housed in a nest of coffins, rather like Russian dolls. Up until the Middle Kingdom, rectangular wooden coffins were used.

Many protective amulets were laid between the wrappings. The Eye of Horus and the scarab were the most popular (see pages 92–93, Amulets). The heart scarab protected the dead person during the Weighing of the Heart ceremony. It was inscribed with a spell.

"Do not stand against me as witness! Do not oppose me in the tribunal! Do not tilt the scales to my disadvantage, in the presence of the Guardian of the Balance."
(See pages 76–77, Weighing of the Heart)

Before burying the mummy, the Opening of the Mouth ceremony was performed. A priest recited spells while touching the mummy's mask with different implements to restore the senses. Only then could the Ka and Ba be at home in the dead person's mummy.

The entire process of mummifying a body was designated to take 70 days. First all the internal organs were removed, except the heart, which was valued for determining thoughts and emotions, and therefore essential in the afterlife. The brains were hooked out through the nose and discarded as useless. But the liver, lungs, intestines and stomach were preserved separately in a set of Canopic jars shaped as the Four Sons of Horus. The body was covered in natron for 40 days, by which time it was suitably desiccated. Aromatic oils and spices were then used to soften the body before padding it out with resin-soaked material to make it more lifelike. Finally, it was wrapped in many layers of linen strips torn from old sheets and clothing. The wealthy often procured the old raiments of the gods from the temples for their mummy wrappings. A lifelike face mask made of cartonnage helped the Ka recognize its own body.

Afterlife

Inside every mummy case was a dead body preserved from decay and wrapp
believed they could only have an everlasting life if the soul could return to the

**Make a bookmark. Color the picture of the mummy. Glue onto cardboard and
Label each drawing on the back of the bookmark.**

Egyptian Mummy

Image of dead person's face

winged scarab beetle
with solar disc

eyes of Horus
symbol of protection

Nut
sky goddess

Horus
falcon god of the sky

ankh
symbol of life

djed pillar
symbol of strength

four sons of Horus

hieroglyphic spell
for dead person's soul

Anubis
jackal god of the dead

Apis bull

Teachers Notes

Illustrations on page 75 are taken from the Book of the Dead – a set of approximately 200 spells with illustrations on papyri. It was placed in the coffin and was designed to guide the Ba safely through the Underworld. The activities, encouraging students to envisage the perils encountered, can be used as source material for an illustrated story or board game.

Extension

1. Compare the journey of the Night Sun with that of the Ba in the Underworld (see pages 66–67, Ra the Sun God).

2. Devise a board game, or write a story or drama, "The Journey through the Underworld."

The Underworld was imagined as a narrow valley with a river running through, similar to Egypt. It was entered through a mountain pass beyond the western horizon. Gates, guarded by demons, led to each of the 42 regions, the same as in Egypt. The Ba had to give the correct password before entering and could only cross the Lake of Dawn and the Winding Water after naming the ferryman and all the parts of his boat. The Ba could call on the gods for strength to overcome its enemies.

> "I shall have power in my heart, I shall have power in my arms, I shall have power in my legs. I shall have power to do whatever I desire."

The Book of the Dead provided everything necessary for reaching the afterlife, including a written confession to be presented at the Hall of Judgment, ensuring no one need ever be found guilty. So, although death was awesome, any Egyptian could be sure of an afterlife of eternal joy, provided appropriate preparations had been made and correct procedures followed.

Egyptians believed that when a person died several souls left the body. One of them was the Ba, which was like a bird with a human head. It was free to fly wherever it liked during the daytime. At night it returned to the tomb.

First the Ba had a most dangerous journey to make through the Underworld. It was given a "Book of the Dead" with a set of spells to protect it from demons and terrible ordeals.

Here is a spell for driving back a crocodile.

> "Get back! Retreat! Get back, you dangerous one! O you with a spine who would work your mouth against this magic of mine."

Naming a demon gave the Ba powerful protection.

> "I know the name of this serpent which is in the mountain. Its name is 'He who is in the burning'."

These are some of the ordeals the Ba faced.

· Crossing a lake of fire

· Being bitten by snakes

· Losing one's heart or head

· Escaping from a fisherman's net

· Being forced to walk upside down

 On a separate piece of paper write other ordeals you can think of.

 On a separate piece of paper draw a picture of this demon.

There were many gateways in the Underworld and the Ba had to name the guards before he was allowed to pass through them. These were some of the names.

· Lord of Knives

· Wallower in Slime

· Clawed One

· Hippo Faced

· He Who Lives on Snakes

What other names can you think of?

_____

_____

_____

_____

Write a spell to protect the Ba from this Mule-eating Serpent.

_____

_____

_____

_____

_____

Teachers Notes

Students can deduce the name of the characters by referring to the passage.

Extension

1. Look in books for examples of illustrations from different books of the dead.

2. Use the picture on the activity sheet to make a wall display. Each student could choose one of the characters and scale it up (x 10), using a grid (See page 79). Choose authentic colors. Cut out characters and assemble. Attach the artist's name, written vertically in hieroglyphs, next to each of the characters (see pages 100–101, Codebreaker). To be consistent with the original painting, the display can be extended to include Osiris sitting in judgment, as shown on page 79.

Hunefer was a royal scribe during the reign of Sethos 1. The picture of the Hall of Judgment has been taken from Hunefer's Book of the Dead, drawn and painted on a papyrus scroll.

The image of Osiris, God of the Underworld is an extension of this illustration in Hunefer's Book of the Dead.

Read about the ceremony of the Weighing of the Heart then label the picture with the words in bold print.

Is Hunefer worthy of a life of eternal joy? Having made the dangerous journey through the Underworld, **Hunefer** reaches the Hall of Two Truths. He kneels before the **jury of judges** and pleads that he has committed no crimes in his life. **Anubis**, the jackal-headed god of the dead, leads Hunefer to the scales to weigh his **heart** against the **Feather of Truth**. He steadies the plumb-bob while **Ammit**, the monstrous Heart Eater, waits to gobble up Hunefer's heart if it is found to weigh heavy with sin. **Thoth**, the ibis-headed god, records the verdict. Then Hunefer is lead away by **Horus** to meet Osiris, God of the Underworld, who will pass the final judgment.

 What questions might the judges have asked Hunefer? Make a list.

1. _____

2. _____

3. _____

4. _____

5. _____

Teachers Notes

The image of Osiris sitting in judgment can be used to extend the picture of the Weighing of the Heart (see page 79).

Extension

1. Read the story of Osiris, his brother Seth and his wife.

2. Make a small Osiris bed. Keep it moist until the grain has sprouted.

3. Consider the parallels between Christianity and the Osiris myth.

Osiris was the first god king of the Egyptians. He brought civilization to Egypt. He taught his people to domesticate animals and cultivate plants. As god of fertility he made the crops grow. His sister and wife, the goddess Isis, taught people how to make bread and beer from grain and to spin and weave linen from flax.

Osiris was murdered by Seth, his jealous brother, who chopped him up and scattered his body across Egypt. Isis found the pieces and, with help from Anubis, put him back together. When he was resurrected he became god of the underworld.

Osiris was the first mummy made by Anubis, God of the Dead and patron of embalmers. Osiris is usually depicted in his white mummy wrappings with hands poking out holding the crook and flail used by farmers. He wears a tall white crown flanked by ostrich feathers. His skin may be black, the color of the fertile silt, or green, the color of sprouting corn, both in keeping with his position as an early god of fertility.

People made small clay figures in the shape of Osiris and embedded them with silt and grain. The seeds germinated and a miniature field in the shape of the god appeared. It symbolized regeneration and was a ritual for encouraging a good harvest. Similar wooden figures were often placed in tombs, including Tutankhamun's. If apparently dead seed could spring to life, so too could a dead body. It confirmed the Egyptians' hope of resurrection.

The Osiris myth was a perfect analogy of the crop cycle. The harvest represented his death, threshing, his dismemberment, sowing the seed, his burial and sprouting, resurrection. He was worshipped as a god of vegetation or corn god. Pilgrims at Abydos, the cult center of Osiris, buried saucers of grain mixed with rich silt and left them to sprout.

Osiris suffered. He was betrayed, murdered and resurrected. The story of his death and eventual resurrection gave people the hope of eternal life. At first only the king was identified with Osiris. When he died he became Osiris, God of the Underworld. Eventually everyone was able to share the hope of an eternal life of joy and could become Osiris too, provided the appropriate rituals were respected. A dead person was referred to as "Osiris so-and-so," in the same way as we refer to "the late John Brown."

Osiris sits upon his throne in the underworld, ready to pass final judgment on the dead. Isis and her sister stand at his back, supporting him. Osiris wears the white crown of Upper Egypt. He holds a shepherd's crook and harvester's flail.

 Enlarge the grid picture of Osiris.

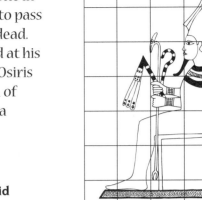

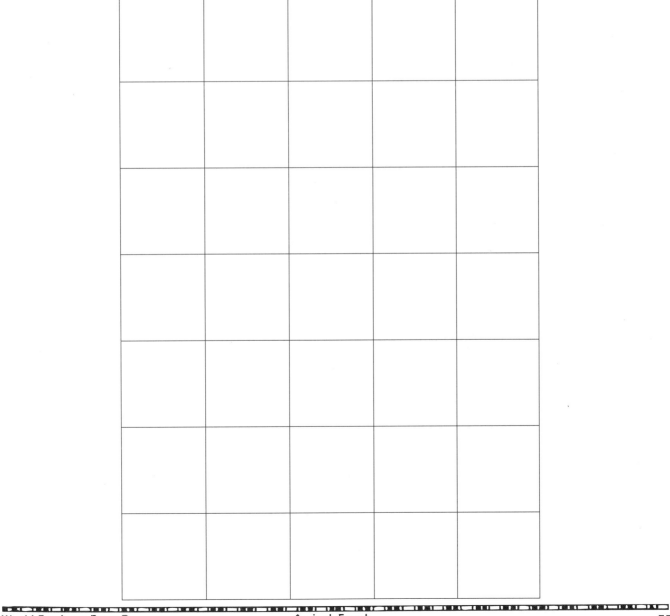

Teachers Notes

A simple model of a tomb can be made by converting a shoe box and adding a cardboard cut-out chapel with a pyramid on top. Make a vaulted roof for the tomb by bending and securing a sheet of cardboard.

For a larger model, use cardboard boxes beneath a table top to indicate above and below ground level. This can provide the context for a display of grave artifacts.

Other model grave goods, such as food and furniture, can be made from modeling clay or cardboard.

Refer to the following pages for:

Funerary Goods

24–25	Nile Boats
44–45	Soul House
72–73	Mummy and Canopic Jars
78–79	Osiris Bed
74–75	Book of the Dead
84–85	Prayer Stela, Shabti and Magic Wand
86–87	Faience Bowls
88–89	Games and Toys
90–99	Jewelry

Wall and Ceiling Decorations

38–39	Harvest Scene
62–63	Craftsmen
64–65	Animal Gods
68–69	Nut the Sky Goddess
100–113	Decorative Hieroglyphs

Extension

1. Some tombs had separate small rooms for different kinds of things, such as a room for musical instruments and another for model boats, each decorated with appropriate wall paintings. Use additional boxes to make rooms opening out from the tomb to house collections of funerary goods.

2. Make a clay statue of the dead person to place in the chapel.

People continued to build small pyramids on top of the roofs of their chapels long after the Age of Pyramids. The Opening of the Mouth funerary ceremony was usually conducted in the chapel courtyard before lowering the mummy into the tomb. The door was then sealed for eternity and the shaft filled with rubble. The chapel was the interface between life and death, where relatives and friends brought food offerings and shared their feast with ancestors on festival days.

Ancient Egyptians spent a lot of time and money preparing for life in the next world. They believed the soul returned to the body each day for food and rest. The dry, rocky hills of the western desert were a perfect place for their cemeteries.

The craftsmen of Deir el-Medina, who made the royal tombs in the Valley of the Kings, cut their own tombs from the rock in the cliffs around their village.

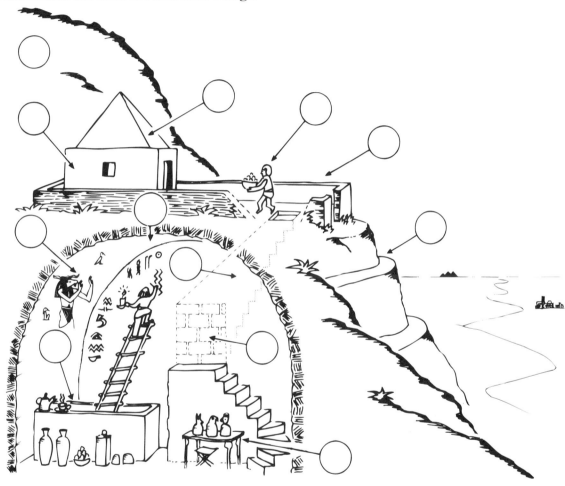

 Label the picture of the tomb at Deir el-Medina.

1. rocky cliff
2. burial chamber
3. wall paintings
4. courtyard
5. mud-brick pyramid
6. path to village
7. offering chapel
8. sealed door
9. sarcophagus
10. burial goods
11. stairs to tomb
12. bringing offerings

 Use the picture to help you make a model of a chapel and tomb. You will need:

- cardboard
- glue
- shoe box
- scissors
- lining paper
- white paint
- tape
- colored pencils

 Decorate your tomb with wall paintings and fill it with treasures for the afterlife.

Teachers Notes

This activity provides an opportunity for students to reflect positively upon their own lives.
The picture is taken from a painting in the tomb of Sennedjem, an overseer from Deir el-Medina.
Make a photocopy enlargement for decorating the wall of the tomb model or use it as a basis for a
wall display.

Observe the following details in the painting:

- The Sun god Ra in his boat attended by adoring baboons
- Opening the mummy's mouth to restore the senses
- Rowing across the lake of death
- Kneeling in adoration of the gods
- Enjoying a rich harvest of corn and flax
- Plowing fields and scattering seed
- Trees and plants bursting with fruit
- Life-giving waters surrounding the fields
- Kneeling before a table laden with offerings

Extension

Look at the pictures of wall paintings in tombs that tell the story of the owner's life on earth and the life
they are looking forward to. Ancient Egyptians appear to have enjoyed themselves for they imagined an
afterlife much like the one they had left behind. Notice how people are nearly always captured in the
prime of life, as they would wish to be for all of eternity. Draw and describe your own life as you would
like to remember it and how you would wish to relive it.

The Field of Reeds was the Egyptians' idea of heaven. They imagined it was like the life they had left behind but free of all troubles. There would be no famine or disease. This was the land of Osiris, god of the Underworld.

Look at the picture of the Fields of Reeds taken from a painting on a tomb wall. Egyptians believed tomb paintings came alive by magic.

Describe how this couple imagined their life after death.

_____

_____

_____

_____

_____

Teachers Notes
This activity provides students with the opportunity to study ancient superstitions and reflect upon modern-day superstitions.

Extension
What are some of the common superstitions and rituals we use to either protect us from bad luck or bring us good luck?

Magic was accepted as part of everyday life in ancient Egypt. Magicians were held in high regard. The goddess Isis was revered for being "great of magic" and was frequently called upon to protect young children. The sage Imhotep, who designed the Step Pyramid, was hailed "The Greatest of Magicians."

Illnesses suspected of being the work of hostile ghosts were attended by doctors who were priests of Sekhmet, the lioness goddess of destruction. Once her rage had been appeased with rituals involving magic spells and potions, it was believed healing could take place.

Magic was invoked to help the dead as well as the living. Protective amulets were enclosed in the mummy wrappings (see pages 92–93, Amulets and 72–73, Mummies).

The Book of the Dead, containing spells to help the Ba on its perilous journey through the Underworld, was an essential funerary item (see page 74–75, Book of the Dead).

Shabtis were small figurines, often in the shape of a mummy, which magically came alive to service the dead. Shabtis can be made from self-hardening clay or hard modeling clay, inscribed with hieroglyphic spells and painted. Brilliant turquoise blue faience shabtis with black line detail were popular (see pages 86–87, Faience Bowls).

> "O Shabti if (name of deceased) be summoned to do any work which has to be done in the realm of the dead – to make arable the fields, to irrigate the land or to convey sand from the west, 'Here am I,' you shall say, 'I shall do it.'"

Stela were limestone prayer tablets, crudely inscribed with a symbol or picture of a chosen deity and signed beneath in hieroglyphs. A picture of an ear, or sometimes rows of ears, ensured the prayer would be heard. Many stela have been found at local shrines around Deir el-Medina. They were also placed in tombs. To make a stela, use plaster of Paris and pour into a prepared mold. Inscribe with a nail. Choose favorite deities or their symbols and include ears. Add a signature written in hieroglyphs (see pages 100–101, Codebreaker). The markings can be highlighted by rubbing with shoe polish or paint.

Magic wands were made of hippopotamus ivory, which supposedly gave them added power. They were used to protect the sleeping and also placed next to mummies to protect the dead. To make a magic wand, use a shaped and sanded piece of thin plywood or, simply, a piece of cardboard. Paint an ivory color and decorate with a black felt-tip pen.

Egyptians believed in magic. Here are some of the things they used for their magical powers.

 Choose one of these objects and make it to actual size.

Prayer Stela or Ear Tablet
Carved from limestone
Height: 10 cm
By speaking into the ear, the worshipper believed the Great Sphinx would be sure to hear the prayer. The stela was signed by the worshipper.

Magic Wand
Made of hippopotamus ivory
Length: 36 cm
Gods and beasts gave the wand power over deadly creatures and evil forces. A line was drawn with the magic wand around the bed at night to protect a sleeping child from snakes and scorpions.

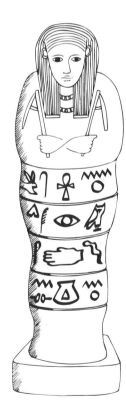

Shabti
Modeled from clay
Height: 10 – 15 cm
Shabtis were little figures of servants that were put in the tomb to help the dead person in the afterlife. Egyptians imagined shabtis came alive and did all the hard work, like digging canals and plowing fields.

Teachers Notes

This activity allows students the opportunity to become familiar with designs and color used in faience bowls.

Extension

1. Make a bowl using a dish as a mold, decorate with blue glaze and black lines in a symmetrical design using fish and lotus flowers.

   You will need:

   - papier-mâché or self-hardening clay
   - black felt-tip pen
   - thick turquoise paint
   - varnish

2. Look for pictures of other things made of faience. The following were popular – flasks, chalices, amulets, shabti figurines and animals including hippopotamus and cat. Choose one of these to make.

3. Make a collection of pottery shards found in gardens or old dumps. What designs do they reveal?

Broken faience and other earthenware was overlooked as worthless by tomb robbers. But fragments do not disintegrate and, 3,000 years later, archaeologists have found and assembled many of these pieces, often revealing exquisite designs.

Faience was made from a glazed quartz compound, usually fashioned in molds. Its typically brilliant blue color pleasingly imitated turquoise and lapis lazuli gemstones. Fish and lotus flower designs were popular and appropriate to the strong blue glaze reminiscent of water. Lotus flowers open with the rising Sun and were symbolic of resurrection. A creation myth describes how the newborn Sun rose out of a lotus as it opened.

Faience is the name given to turquoise blue glazed earthenware, usually with a black painted design. Egyptians used it to mold all manner of things.

Archaeologists have learned a great deal about ancient Egypt by piecing together fragments of earthenware found in tombs and households.

 Cut out these fragments from two different faience bowls. Piece them together and complete the designs.

Teachers Notes

This activity provides students with the opportunity to play the ancient game of Senet.

Extension

1. Find out what pastimes Egyptians enjoyed. Look at pictures of paintings on papyri and tomb walls for evidence. Chariot hunting, fowling, fishing, acrobatics, wrestling, dancing, playing music, partying and feasting were all popular.

2. Find out about children's toys and the games they played. Mechanical wooden toys were common. They were operated by levers or string, or pulled along on wheels. Children also had spinning tops, juggling balls and dolls. Make a mechanical toy similar to ones Egyptian children played with, such as a hippopotamus on wheels or a crocodile with jaws that open and close.

Senet was also known as the game of 30 squares. It was often played on a simple grid scratched on stone. More elaborate sets were made in black ebony wood, with ivory inlay and drawers beneath to contain the playing pieces. Several games of senet were among the treasures in Tutankhamun's tomb.

Senet was the most popular game in Egypt. It was played by young and old, and put in tombs of the dead to play in the afterlife.

 Mark out the game board, stick down black paper strips and decorate with hieroglyphs as shown. Make five black and five white playing pieces from clay. Make throwing sticks from balsa wood by rounding off one side of each stick with sandpaper. To make your own game you will need:

- thick white cardboard 35 cm x 11 cm
- four strips of balsa wood 1 x 1 – 6 cm long
- self-hardening clay
- black and white acrylic paint
- strips of black paper
- small box for playing pieces

- paintbrush
- glue
- felt-tip pens
- scissors
- sandpaper

How to play:

The skill is in defending your pieces while blocking your opponent's.

1. Set up board as shown and move in the direction of the arrows.
2. Score with throwing sticks – flat side up = 1, 2 flat sides up = 2, etc.
3. Move piece onto empty square or swap places with an opponent's piece.
4. Two pieces of the same color next to each other cannot be attacked.
5. Three pieces of the same color next to each other cannot be attacked or overtaken.
6. All throws must be used. Move backwards if no pieces can be moved forward.
7. Squares with hieroglyphs are safe from attack.

   ⌂ All pieces must land here with an exact throw before moving on.

   ≈ If a piece lands here return to square with an ankh ☥ but if occupied return to the beginning.

8. An exact throw is needed to exit from any of the last three squares.

To start:

The first player to throw a "1" moves the last black piece down onto the second row and throws again.

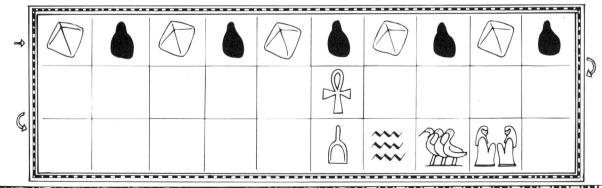

Teachers Notes

Egyptian jewelry is very symbolic and an understanding of these symbols is essential to understanding Egyptian culture. This activity provides students with the opportunity to develop this understanding.

Extension

1. Look in books to find examples of other royal jewelry. Identify some of the magic symbols used, such as a lotus flower or cobra.

2. Make a pectoral of the winged scarab (see page 91).

A pectoral is an elaborate form of the pendant and was worn hanging from either a simple bead necklace or a strap of beadwork, adjusted to fall just below a broad collar (see page 95).

Tutankhamun's pectoral symbolizes the birth of the Sun and the Moon, and illustrates the amuletic nature of Egyptian jewelry. Every detail is symbolic. The scarab represents Khepri, the Sun god at dawn, and is shown supporting a celestial bark or boat containing symbols of the Sun and Moon. The small figures at the top are Thoth the Moon god, with the king, both facing Ra the Sun god. A cobra with a sun disc is a protector of royalty. A lotus flower symbolizes resurrection and is a popular motif in all kinds of jewelry.

Tomb robbers ransacked nearly every tomb in the Valley of the Kings searching for gold and jewels, but they overlooked some of the jewelry in Tutankhamun's horde of treasures.

This gold ornament, called a pectoral, was found in his tomb. He probably wore it at his coronation. It is made of gold and inlaid with semi-precious stones. The scarab beetle at the center is carved from a pale green gemstone. The other stones are:

lapis lazuli – deep blue for protection
turquoise – blue-green for joy
carnelian – blood-red for power

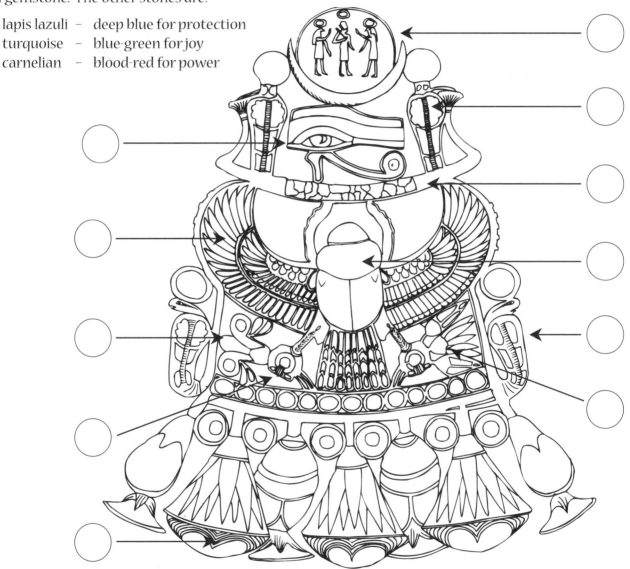

Read the description then number the different parts of the ornament.
Color it with the colors of semi-precious stones.

At the center of the ornament is a (**1**) carved scarab with the (**2**) wings of a falcon. Its talons are gripping the (**3**) shen rings of eternity. In one is the (**4**) papyrus flower of Lower Egypt and in the other (**5**) lotus flowers of Upper Egypt. It is protected on either side by (**6**) cobras with solar discs. The scarab supports a (**7**) celestial bark with the (**8**) eye of Horus and two more (**9**) cobras with solar discs. At the top is a (**10**) crescent Moon and disc with the King, Tutankhamun, the Moon god, Thoth and the Sun god, Ra. Beneath the scarab hang (**11**) lotus buds and flowers.

Teachers Notes

This activity provides students with the opportunity to study ancient charms and reflect upon modern-day charms.

Extension

1. Scarab Seal
   Make a scarab seal using self-hardening clay or hard modeling clay. Inscribe the base using a ballpoint tip with a cartouche of your own name. Use an ink pad to make prints with the seal.

2. Consider the meaning of some of the symbols we use – cross, horseshoe, owl, black cat, heart, red rose.

Jewelry was worn for protection as well as adornment. People always tied charms of clay or stone around their necks and wrists to impart particular power, or for protection from hostile forces, which could otherwise cause misfortune. Miniature images of gods or goddesses were common and everyone had their favorite. Animals were also popular for their different qualities, such as a lion for courage or a bull for strength. Some hieroglyphic shapes were symbolic and used for their magical power.

1. The Eye of Horus was also known as the "Wadjet" eye. Horus was a falcon god and his markings are that of a falcon's left eye. It was torn out by his uncle Seth during a fight to avenge his father's murder, but was magically restored by the goddess Hathor and so the Eye of Horus came to symbolize "making whole," the literal sense of healing. It survives to this day as a popular symbol for bestowing protection from the evil eye.

2. The ankh is thought to derive from the shape of a sandal strap. It represents life-giving air and water and is a powerful symbol of life. The gods always carried the ankh and are often depicted presenting it to the king, thereby conferring upon him a divine and eternal life.

3. The scarab is a symbol of self-creation and resurrection. The winged scarab and heart scarab were specifically funerary amulets used to protect the mummy in the afterlife (see pages 66–67, Ra the Sun God).

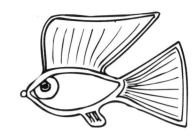

Amulets are like good luck charms. Egyptians wore them to protect themselves from dangers and dark forces. Children often wore fish pendants in their hair to protect them from drowning in the river.

Here are three of the most popular symbols worn as amulets.

 Look in books to find out what each symbol means and why people wore them.

Eye of Horus

meaning: _____

_____

_____

worn because: _____

_____

Ankh

meaning: _____

_____

_____

worn because: _____

_____

Scarab Beetle

meaning: _____

_____

_____

worn because: _____

_____

Choose one of these symbols and make an amulet to wear as a pendant.
  You will need:

- cardboard
- felt-tip pens
- scissors
- colored paper
- cord
- sequins
- glue
- buttons, etc. for gems

Teachers Notes
The collar could be enlarged by photocopying or the pattern could be simplified – look at different collars.

Extension
1. Order of the Golden Collar
   Make a heavy necklace of gold beads from self-hardening clay or hard modeling clay. Shape on a knitting needle and paint with gold acrylic paint.

2. Bracelet, Armlet and Anklet
   Use strips of cardboard approximately 6 cm wide, fastened with string ties. Decorate in imitation of strings of beads, similar to the broad collar, possibly with a large central amulet, such as a scarab, set between strings of beads.

3. Bangle
   Make a bangle using papier-mâché wrapped around a hoop of cardboard. Paint either gold or ivory and inscribe with hieroglyphs using a black felt-tip pen (see Hieroglyph section).

A broad collar was the most characteristic piece of Egyptian jewelry and was worn as an item of clothing.

Since predynastic times, necklaces of shells, stones or faience beads had been included in even the poorest burials. Several such necklaces, skillfully strung together, could be arranged to form a collar. Most popular were cylindrical beads strung vertically with a lower row of drop beads, secured using crescent shaped end pieces.

Some funerary collars were shaped from sheet gold in the form of a vulture, with outstretched wings forming a semicircle.

There were also collars of natural garlands made by sewing rows of petals, leaves and berries onto papyrus.

The earliest bangles were made from sections of ivory tusks and later from gold. Bangles were often inscribed with a good luck wish in hieroglyphs or a cartouche of the reigning king.

Men and women wore broad collars of beads.
The king awarded collars of gold beads to his favorite officials.

 Make your own collar using the pattern below.
Look in books to find ideas for different designs.

You will need:

- felt-tip pens
- string or cord
- tape
- strong paper
- colored paper
  (maroon, turquoise, green, black and gold)

- cardboard
- scissors
- stapler
- compass

reinforce hinge with tape

◀ attach end piece here ▶

1. Mark a semicircle for the collar using a compass. Scale up two times (1:2).

2. Make two end pieces from folded paper.

3. Cut out and decorate with felt-tip pens or shapes cut from colored paper.

4. Attach end pieces to collar with staples.

5. Fasten with cord or string.

Teachers Notes

Students are provided with the opportunity to make their own diadems or crowns and develop an understanding of their use.

Extension

Create a diadem to suit their own personality – use items that represent things that are personally important to them. These diadems can then be displayed with an explanation of the items represented. Other students in the class can guess which student made which diadem.

The royal crown of princess Sit-Hathor-Yunet was made from a broad band of sheet gold with a plume at the back and streamers hinged on roundels (round flower designs) at either side. The roundels were inlaid with lapis lazuli, turquoise and carnelian. Wigs were often worn on special occasions and were made from either black wool or human hair.

When the gusty north wind was blowing, boatmen kept their hair in place with a strip of linen or water weed tied around their brow. On festival days they tucked lotus flowers into their hair.

Jewelers copied the boatman's circlet and made diadems using gold strips or wire decorated with rosettes of red, green and blue inlay.

 Use the designs on this sheet to help you make your own diadem.

You will need:

- cardboard
- scissors
- gold paper
- black and gold pens
- wire
- glue
- black yarn
- gold braid
- colored paper (red, blue and green)
- paper fasteners (for attaching roundels)

You could use natural materials instead (leaves, flowers, berries and twining plants like ivy).

Royal Crown

The diadem became a royal crown when the symbol of a cobra was added.

Here is the crown and wig of Princess Sit-Hathor-Yunet.

The round flower designs are called roundels. This roundel is based on the rush flower.

Gold tubes have been threaded onto the locks of hair.

Teachers Notes

Having an understanding of Egyptian headdresses, students are then presented with the opportunity to make a Vulture Headdress for themselves. This design will need to be enlarged to double the size.

Extension

1. Make a Nemes Cloth

    Typically worn by kings, this is the headdress represented on the familiar gold mask of Tutankhamun.

    Use a piece of sheet, striped blue and yellow with fabric crayons. Pull back across the forehead and behind the ears and secure at the back. Cut the side flaps to shape so they fall over the shoulders. Gather at the back into a pigtail. Decorate the brow with a royal vulture cut from paper and reinforced with wire.

2. Eye Makeup

    Look carefully at pictures showing how Egyptians used eyeliner. Use black eyeliner for the same effect.

    Both men and women wore makeup. They used kohl for drawing a strong black line around the eyes. Lips and cheeks were painted with red clay or with rust-red iron oxide mixed with oil. Henna was used to redden hair as well as palms and soles. Perfume was made from oil scented with cinnamon and myrrh. Mirrors, often in the shape of a lotus flower, were made from polished silver or copper.

This headdress was worn by queens. The vulture represented the goddess Nekhbet of Upper Egypt who, as a protector of royalty, was portrayed in all kinds of royal regalia.

Pictures of Cleopatra usually show her wearing a vulture headdress made of beaten gold.

 Use the design below to make the vulture headdress.

fold

You will need:

- scissors

- wire

- glue

- tape

- brown felt-tip pen

- gold crayon

- thin cardboard for template

- sheet of heavy paper

How to make:

1. Make a template of the above picture scaled up three times (1:3).

2. Cut out from heavy paper.

3. Draw feather patterns with felt-tip pen and color with gold crayon.

4. Bend and tape together.

5. Stick two sides of the vulture head together, opening outwards at the fold.

6. Fold tailpiece.

7. Attach head and tail to headdress.

Teachers Notes

This page introduces just a few of the 500 hieroglyphs in regular use that correspond to our alphabet. The decorative surround is based on a classic design used around doorways in tombs. The winged sun disc is a symbol of Horus the sky god (see pages 64–65, Animal Gods).

Extension

1. Find examples in books of the different ways hieroglyphs were used in ancient Egypt.
   These may include:
   - Carved on stone obelisks, statues and temple walls;
   - Painted on mummy cases and tomb walls;
   - Drawn on funerary papyri;
   - Incised on scarab seals and amulets; or
   - Inlaid with semi-precious stones in furniture and jewelry.

2. Find out how papyrus was made and used. Draw a series of diagrams to illustrate the process.
   Sheets of papyrus were made from the pith inside the stalks of the reed. It was cut into strips, laid at right angles, beaten flat and then dried. Black soot and red ochre were used as ink pigments. The reed pen was cut in a wedge shape, like a calligraphy pen.

3. Compare examples of different ancient scripts.
   Identify samples of Roman, Greek and Babylonian scripts.

Each hieroglyph is a small, distinct picture or sign. Although each one may have originally stood for a whole word, the meaning was not necessarily related to the image at all but could represent a sound or an idea. This was most confusing for those attempting to decipher hieroglyphs. For hundreds of years, travelers were to gaze in wonderment, perplexed at the hidden meaning of the signs they found on the walls of abandoned tombs and temple ruins. All kinds of mysteries were attributed to the carvings, and since they bore no resemblance to anything familiar, it was postulated that an alien race had been at work, an idea persisting to the present day.

Egyptians believed the god Thoth gave people the power of writing. He taught them the sacred signs which we call hieroglyphs. Some are like pictograms, others represent ideas and many have sounds which are put together to make words. The hieroglyphs on this sheet have similar sounds to letters in our alphabet.

Label the hieroglyphs using the words below. Some are done for you.

water	hand	chick	basket	owl	hill	mouth
bread	reed	eagle	serpent	leg	lion	rope

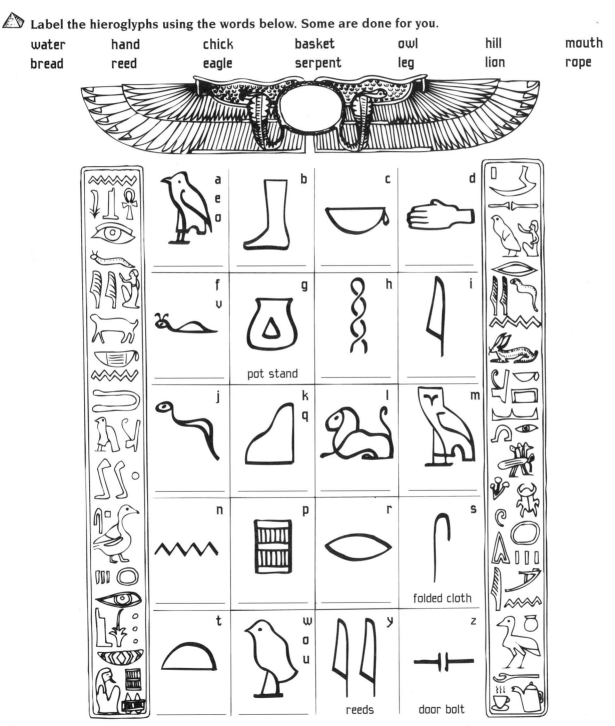

Practice drawing the above hieroglyphs on a separate piece of paper and write a secret message. If you need a letter which is not included, use this sign: ø.

Teachers Notes

The exercises on this page replicate the steps taken by Jean Francois Champollion, a gifted linguist, who, in 1822, unraveled the mystery of hieroglyphs, after 14 years of research.

Extension

1. Look in books for a picture of the Rosetta stone.

2. Make bookmarks with personalized cartouches using the hieroglyphs on page 103. Take care to arrange the hieroglyphs attractively.

Champollian had been attached to an expedition led by Napoleon, who was also fascinated by the wonders of ancient Egypt. The Rosetta stone was the key. It was inscribed with hieroglyphs and beneath were translations in demotic script and also ancient Greek. Champollian was able to read the Greek names of Ptolemy, Cleopatra and Alexander and deduce that signs within the cartouches spelled out the names of royalty. He then translated the Egyptian hieroglyphs phonetically from the Greek. Having made this great breakthrough, he proceeded to decipher other cartouches inscribed on temple walls, which was more difficult since the hieroglyphs for the names of Egyptian kings carried additional symbolic meaning (see the inscription for Thutmose on page 103).

Names of kings and queens were written inside a coiled piece of rope called a cartouche. Here are some examples. The first and second cartouche have been translated. Each hieroglyph makes the sound of the letter beneath.

🔺 **Using this information, decipher the name in the third cartouche opposite.**

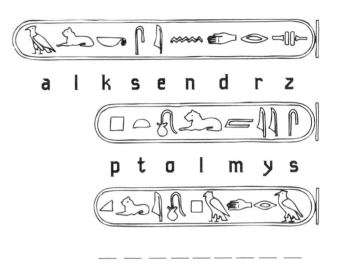

a l k s e n d r z

p t o l m y s

_ _ _ _ _ _ _ _

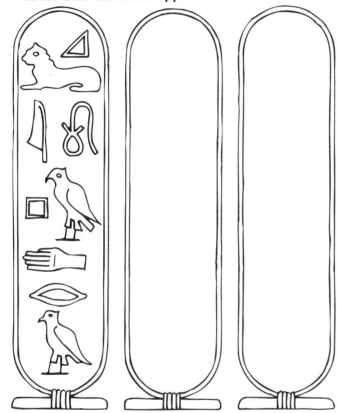

Hieroglyphs can be written from top to bottom like the one opposite. Notice how the hieroglyphs have been carefully arranged.

🔺 **Complete the other cartouches for Ptolmys and Alexander.**

Hieroglyphs can also be written from right to left as well as left to right. Below is a decorative cartouche for King Thutmose with sacred inscriptions.

Note: Daughter of Ra is written

🔺 **On a separate piece of paper make an inscription like the one above with your name inside the cartouche.**

Teachers Notes

Compare the plants and animals of the Nile valley to those once common in your locality.

Extension

Make your own pictograms to reflect the modern-day world you live in.

Egyptians believed hieroglyphs had a life of their own and that depicting dangerous animals, like crocodiles, could have dire consequences, unless they were disempowered by drawing them mutilated.

Many hieroglyphs are pictures of plants and animals once common in the Nile Valley.

Color and number these hieroglyphs.

1. oryx
2. duckling
3. egret catching fish
4. crocodile
5. heron
6. lamb
7. chicks in a nest
8. swallow
9. rabbit
10. lotus bud
11. papyrus clump
12. lotus flower
13. vulture
14. ape
15. three reeds
16. lizard
17. turtle
18. two sedge
19. beetle
20. scorpion
21. flamingo
22. fish
23. bee
24. palm tree

Teachers Notes

A tally of numbers could be recorded on a slate. Write inventories using a dip pen made from a sharpened stick and "papyrus" made from tea-stained sheets of paper. Use the Egyptian number system and devise pictograms for different things like tables and chairs.

Extension

Make inventories for the following:

(a) Farmers' livestock-
835 long-horned cattle, 220 short-horned cattle, 760 donkeys, 974 sheep, 2,234 goats.

(b) Spoils of war-
prisoners, horses, chariots, cattle, sheep

(c) Nobleman's storehouse-
rolls of fine linen, pots of honey, jars of wine and oil, bricks of salt, leopard skins, gold collars.

(d) Gifts paid out from the royal treasury to the temples during the reign of Rameses III.

2,382,605	various fruits	6,272,421	loaves of bread
19,130,032	bouquets of flowers	1,933,766	jars of oil
1,075,635	amulets of precious stones	5,279,652	sacks of corn

Scribes were highly regarded in ancient Egypt. They were very important because they were responsible for keeping records of everything. They performed a census each year, where all people and livestock in every village were recorded. The scribes recorded all taxes paid to the king and kept up-to-date inventories of Egyptian storerooms.

Scribes kept records of everything. Each year a census was taken in every village of all the people and the livestock. Taxes paid to the king were carefully recorded. Storeroom inventories were kept up to date. Opposite are hieroglyphs for the numbers scribes used. For example:

1 =)

10 = ∩

100 = ℮

1,000 = ⚱

10,000 = 𓆐

100,000 = 𓁨

1,000,000 = 𓁨

17 is written ∩ ////

2,132 is written ⚱⚱ ℮ ∩∩ //

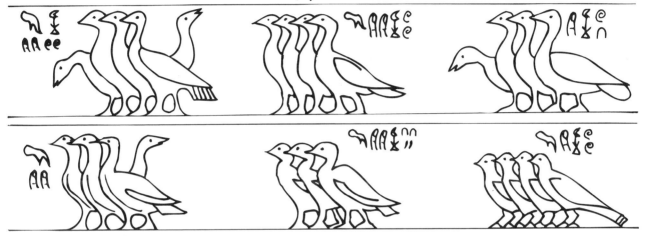

🔺 **Look at the picture recording all the fowls on a nobleman's estate. Complete the inventory for the different species. The first one is done for you.**

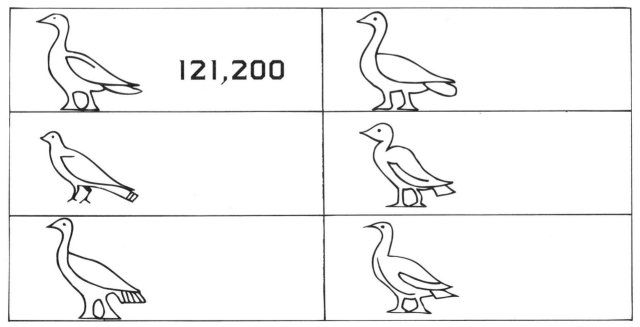

121,200

During the reign of Rameses III, the temple of Amun in Thebes was very wealthy. It owned 65 towns, 46 workshops, 86,486 serfs, 433 orchards, 691,334 acres of land and 421,362 cattle.

🔺 **Make an inventory on a separate piece of paper like the one above to record the wealth of the temple.**

🔺 **Make an inventory for some of the things in your class on a separate piece of paper.**

Teachers Notes

The picture shows the taxman "stretching the cord" while the farmer and his wife approach bearing gifts, which could be construed as bribes!

Extension

1. Mark out foundations for a building of a given size by "stretching the cord." Using the knotted string make 3, 4, 5 triangles to determine right angle corners for the foundations.

2. Calculate tax demands.
   If the grain tax is 20% of the crop and the expected yield is two sacks of grain per setat, how much tax will the farmer pay if he has 10 setats, 20 setats, etc.?

3. Roughly estimate the following lengths in metric measurement.
   - alabaster statue – 13 cubits
   - obelisk – 120 cubits high
   - boat – 60 cubits long and 30 cubits wide

4. The solar bark buried alongside the Great Pyramid of Khufu at Giza is 43 meters long. Approximately what length is this in cubits?

5. The Great Sphinx at Giza measures 73 meters long and 20 meters high. Approximately what does it measure in cubits?

The ancient Egyptians devised their own method of measuring the length, height and area of objects.

A cubit is the equivalent of the length of the arm from the elbow to the tip of the middle finger, which is approximately equal to 52.4 cm.

A palm is the width of the hand with the thumb held over the inside of the palm.

A digit is the width of one finger.

Egyptians measured length in cubits, palms and digits.

 Look at the diagram and complete the following.

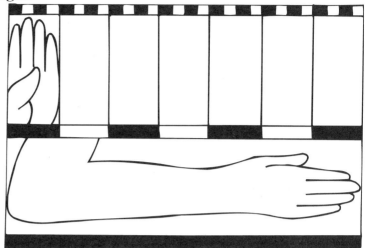

1 cubit = ☐ palms

1 palm = ☐ digits

1 cubit = ☐ digits

 Use your own arm to mark out a cubit. Compare it to the royal cubit of 52.4 cm.

What is the difference? _____

 Make a measuring rod from a piece of card using the royal cubit. Mark it off in palms and digits.

Use it for measuring different lengths, e.g., door height. Record your findings.

height of door	

Taxmen visited every farm each year to survey the fields and find the total area of land being cultivated. They then estimated the size of the crops and calculated the farmer's tax demand.

Strips of farmland were marked out by "stretching the cord." Each strip was called a setat. It was one cubit wide and one hundred cubits long. So one setat = one hundred square cubits.

 Make an Egyptian cord by knotting a piece of string at intervals of a cubit. "Stretch the cord" and find the number of setats in the school field or playground. Draw a plan on a separate piece of paper to show the area in setats.

Teachers Notes

These pages provide opportunity for artwork producing decorative borders using different media and materials.

Extension

1. Decorate a cut-out stone obelisk shape with hieroglyphs arranged vertically.

2. Make a sacred doorway surround using decorative hieroglyphs with a protective winged sun disk across the top (see page 101, Codebreaker).

The hieroglyph of a seated woman was used to qualify anything feminine, such as a woman's name. Similarly, a seated man was placed after hieroglyphs denoting a man's name.

Sailing upstream was a synonym for south and a boat drifting downstream was a synonym for north.

Make a set of "print blocks."

You will need:

- string
- scissors
- glue
- roller
- paint
- four cardboard squares (8 – 10 cm²)

1. Follow the steps for drawing hieroglyphs.
2. Draw each one on a cardboard square.
3. Cut pieces of string and glue down along the line of drawing.
4. Use a roller to apply paint to the print block.
   Be careful not to overload the print block with paint.
5. Use your print blocks to make patterns and borders.

twisted rope

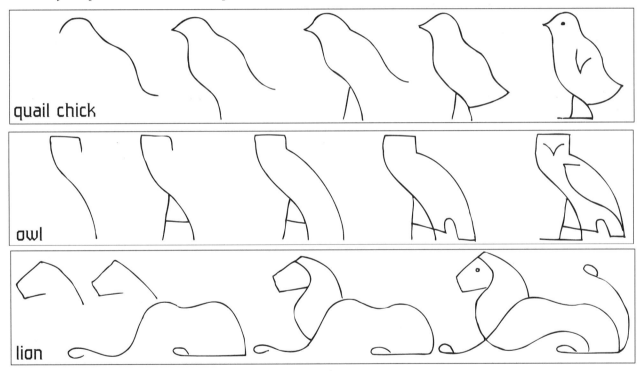

quail chick

owl

lion

Hieroglyphs were often beautifully decorated like the ones below.

 Decorate and color some of your own hieroglyphs.

See page 110 for Printing and Silhouettes background information and teachers notes.

Ancient Egypt

Hieroglyphs were sometimes painted like silhouettes. Cut out the hieroglyphs and arrange them carefully, cover with thin paper then make rubbings of them with the side of a crayon.

woman

duckling

tree

boat sailing upstream

Make your own templates using these hieroglyphs.

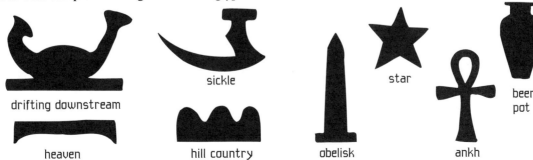

drifting downstream

sickle

heaven

hill country

obelisk

star

ankh

beer pot

Teachers Notes

"Necessity, the mother of invention." Consider how inventions arise from necessity and opportunity.

Extension

1. Trace the line of development of these early inventions to the form they use today.

2. Research and discuss modern-day inventions.

Egyptian civilization depended on many of the advances made by early settlers in the Near East. Their ideas and inventions were spread by migrants and traders across the ancient world. When people in the Nile Valley were still roaming in bands, early settlers elsewhere were building with mud bricks and plowing the land.

Necessity and opportunity prompted early farmers to invent all manner of things. Their settled way of life, unlike the roaming hunters and gatherers before them, meant they were able to accumulate possessions, and also build more substantial dwellings, improvising with whatever materials the locality offered – mud, straw, reeds, or timber.

Clay pots and baskets were made for storing grain and other food crops safe from pests. Hair and wool, collected from domesticated animals, provided the raw material for woven cloth. Discovering how to raise the temperature of a furnace with bellows made it possible to cast metal and so advance the design of farming implements and weapons.

As trade developed, sturdy wooden boats were needed for transporting heavy cargoes across the sea. Writing emerged with the need to keep records of merchandise.

See the following activity sheets for background information on different inventions:

Casting Metal – pages 62–63, Archaeological Evidence

Writing – pages 100–113, Hieroglyphs section

Domesticating animals – pages 46–47, Domesticated Animals

Brickmaking – pages 62–63, Archaeological Evidence

Irrigation – pages 28–29, Irrigation

Plowing – pages 32–35, Calendar Wheel

Baking Bread – pages 48–49, Food

Boatbuilding – pages 24–27, Nile Boats and Papyrus Skiff

Spread of Agriculture – pages 32–43, Farmers' Year

Wild animals once roamed across grassy plains of North Africa. Then, about 10,000 years ago, the climate changed and the green plains turned to desert. Nomadic hunters moved down to the river valley. They settled in villages. Life was very different, however, and they had much to learn. Over many years, they found out all kinds of things that helped them change their way of life.

Here are some of the things they learned:

- boatbuilding
- irrigating fields
- making pottery
- baking bread
- casting metal

- plowing
- writing
- grinding corn
- basket making

- spinning and weaving
- domesticating animals
- building with mud bricks
- fishing with nets

 Color, cut out and label the pictures using the list above to help you. Think about how these different inventions might have come about. Glue them on a separate piece of paper and write a sentence to explain each picture.

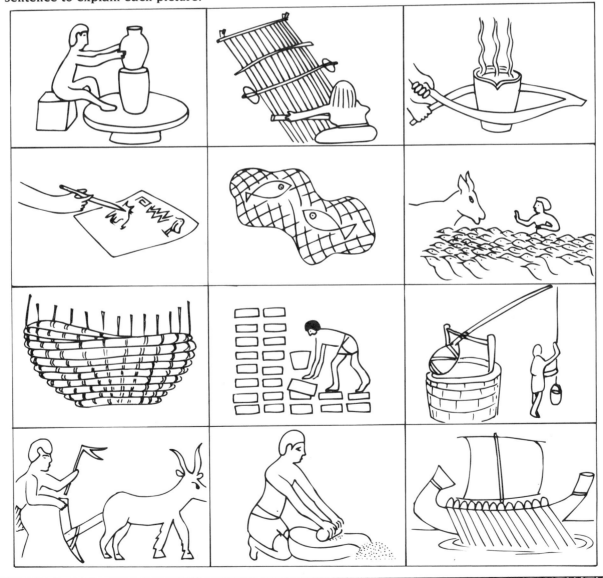

Teachers Notes

The following brief account of Egypt's history corresponds to and amplifies the sequence of key events illustrated and described in the Timeline activity sheets.

The pictures and labels can be enlarged and pegged in sequence along a string denoting a timeline using the information below. Students need pages 117 and 119 to complete the timeline.

Extension

Students make a timeline representing their own life.

1. Lower Egypt was once split into several city states around the Delta and was relatively wealthy compared to the farming communities of Upper Egypt, along the banks of the Nile. But Upper Egypt was more united (see Farmers' Year – Introduction).

2. Princes and local chieftains controlled Egypt until around 3000 B.C. when a legendary leader of the south, called Menes, made a political takeover of the north and unified the whole country. He wore the double crown: the white crown of Upper Egypt and the red crown of Lower Egypt. He founded the capital city of Memphis, where the Delta joins the river, the junction between the "Two Lands," which to some extent always remained as such, each having its own distinct culture. Menes was apparently killed by a hippopotamus (see pages 56–57, Kings).

3. During the Old Kingdom, the people were protected by the divine power of a king who communed with the gods. It was a golden age of talent and innovation, with unparalleled achievement in architectural design. Imhotep, who designed the Step Pyramid, the first monumental stone building in the world, was a high priest of Heliopolis. He was a healer, sculptor, architect and sage – one of the greatest geniuses of all time and later recognized by the Greeks as the father of medicine (see pages 12–13, Pyramids).

4. After about 500 years of relative peace and security, there followed 100 years of hardship and disunity. There were many kings, each one ruling for only a few years. Then a Theban king, called Mentuhotep II, united the country once again and a new era began.

5. Trade flourished and a string of fortresses along the Nile, south of the border in Nubia, secured Egypt's control of Nubian resources (see Jewelry Section, Introduction).

6. From the East, migrants, called the Hyksos, arrived. They settled in the Delta and introduced new technology, including the horse and chariot. Their control spread throughout Egypt. But eventually Theban princes rose up and evicted the foreign rulers. Their leader, Ahmose, established a new dynasty and so began the New Kingdom.

7. With military skills and sophisticated weaponry acquired from the Hyksos, Thutmose I, first of the warrior pharaohs, begins to establish an empire that extended to the Euphrates in the east and far south into Nubia, "from the Horns of the Earth to the Marshes of Asia" (see pages 18–21, Foreign Trade).

Continued on page 118.

Make a timeline for ancient Egypt. Color, cut out and arrange these pictures and labels in sequence on a long piece of paper according to their chronological order.

8. Hatshepsut is famous for having been the only female pharaoh. She came to power first as a regent but soon declared herself king, to seize the position from her young nephew Thutmose III. She ruled for more than 20 years and was renowned for her fine temples and fabled trading mission to the Land of Punt (see pages 56-57, Kings and pages 18-21, Foreign Trade).

9. Egypt continued to accumulate great wealth from tributes of foreign kings. The Empire was at its height under Thutmose III but then went into decline. Several provinces in the east were lost during the reign of Akhenaten, the "heretic" pharaoh, who was preoccupied with replacing both Thebes and Memphis with a new capital called Akhetaten, dedicated to the one and only god, Aten. Soon after his death the city was abandoned (see pages 14-15, Tutankhamun's Tomb).

10. Tutankhamun, Akhenaten's nephew, reigned briefly, during which time temples were reopened and the old order was re-established (see pages 14-15, Tutankhamun's Tomb).

11. A new dynasty was founded by a family of military generals that included Rameses II, who fought the Hittites to regain some of the lost territories. (see pages 16-17, Abu Simbel).

12. But after Rameses III had fought off the Sea People, the Empire went into a serious decline from which it never recovered.

13. A series of invaders assumed power – Libyans from north Africa, followed by Nubians from the south and then Assyrians and Persians from the east. However, Egypt remained a prosperous country.

14. When Alexander the Great triumphantly marched into Egypt, liberating the country from Persian rule, he was declared son of Amun and pharaoh of Egypt. He founded the capital of Alexandria on the Mediterranean coast, which became a major center of trading. Alexander's general, Ptolemy, established the Ptolemic dynasty that spread Greek culture throughout Egypt. The library of Alexandria, the largest known, became the cultural center of the ancient world. The ancient wisdom of Egypt was to exert a strong influence on the Greeks and later the Romans.

15. Cleopatra VII, at the age of 18, became the final ruler of Egypt. After her first protector, Julius Caesar, had been assassinated she fell in love with a Roman general, Mark Antony. When Octavian of Rome declared war on Egypt, Mark Antony led Cleopatra's troops against the Romans but was defeated at the naval battle of Actium. Rather than be taken captive, both Mark Antony and Cleopatra committed suicide. Cleopatra died from the bite of an asp, a death believed to bestow eternal life.

Egypt became a valuable province, the "bread basket" of the Roman Empire.

Make a timeline for ancient Egypt. Color, cut out and arrange these labels and pictures in sequence on a long piece of paper according to their chronological order.

5000 B.C. Farmers settle in the Nile Valley.

3100 B.C. Menes is crowned "Lord of Two Lands." He is the first king of Upper and Lower Egypt.

2686–2181 B.C.
Old Kingdom

2630 B.C. Imhotep designs the step pyramid for King Djoser at Saqqara. The Age of Pyramids begins.

2181–2040 B.C.
1st Intermediate Period

2135 B.C. Civil war breaks out. Tombs and temples are ransacked. People die of famine.

2040–1633 B.C.
Middle Kingdom

1990 B.C. Egypt conquers Northern Nubia. Fortresses are built along the Nile to defend the gold route through Nubia.

1633–1567 B.C.
2nd Intermediate Period

1640 B.C. The Hyksos invade from the east with horse-drawn chariots. They rule Egypt for over 100 years.

1570–1070 B.C.
New Kingdom

1504 B.C. Thutmose I begins building a mighty empire as far as the Euphrates river. Armies are led to victory by the god Amun of Thebes.

1570–1070 B.C.
New Kingdom

1473 B.C. Hatshepsut, the only ever female pharaoh, sends a trading fleet to Punt. It returns with myrrh trees and baboons.

1570–1070 B.C.
New Kingdom

1345 B.C. Akhenhaten and his wife, Nefertiti, close all the temples. People are only allowed to worship one god – Aten, the Sun god.

1570–1070 B.C.
New Kingdom

1333 B.C. Tutankhamun, the boy king, is crowned king at the age of 8 but rules for only 11 years. He reopens all the temples.

1570–1070 B.C.
New Kingdom

1274 B.C. Rameses II signs the first ever peace treaty with the Hittites after the battle of Qadesh.

1570–1070 B.C.
New Kingdom

1190 B.C. Rameses III, the last warrior king, defeats the "Sea People."

1085–332 B.C.
3rd Intermediate Period

770 B.C. Egypt is overrun by enemies – Nubia, Libya, Assyria and Persia. The empire falls apart.

332–30 B.C.
Ptolemic Period

332 B.C. Alexander the Great from Macedon liberates Egypt from Persian rulers. The Ptolemic dynasty is begun by Ptolemy, one of Alexander's generals.

332–30 B.C.
Ptolemic Period

30 B.C. The Romans invade. Cleopatra VII, last queen of Egypt, commits suicide.

Glossary of Terms

ankh   a T-shaped cross with a loop at the top

cartouche   an oval or oblong figure enclosing characters that represent the name of a sovereign

demotic script   simplified form of writing used in Egypt between 700 B.C. and A.D. 500

faience   glazed earthenware or pottery, esp. a fine variety with highly colored designs

flail   an instrument for threshing grain consisting of a handle on which is attached a free-swinging stick or bar

kohl   a powder, such as finely powdered antimony sulfide, used as a cosmetic

mattock   an instrument for loosening the soil in digging, shaped like a pickax, but having one end broad instead of pointed

natron   a mineral, hydrated sodium carbonate

nilometer   a graduated pillar or other vertical surface, serving as a scale or gauge to indicate the height to which the Nile rises during its annual floods

oryx   a large antelope with long, nearly straight horns

pannier   a basket, esp. a large one for carrying goods or provisions

pulses   edible seeds of certain leguminous plants, as peas, beans or lentils

quern   a primitive hand-operated mill for grinding grain

sarcophagus   a stone coffin, esp. one bearing sculpture and inscriptions

schistosome   a parasite in the blood vessels of humans and other mammals; also known as bilharziasis or snail fever

sedge   any rushlike or grasslike plant, growing in wet places

shadoof (shaduf)   a device used in Egypt for raising water, esp. for irrigation, consisting of a long suspended rod with a bucket at one end and a weight at the other

vizier   a high official in certain countries, esp. a minister of state